TO HAVE & TO HOLD

*Dedicated to the memory of
Preb. Austen Williams CVO
(1912–2001)*

TO HAVE & TO HOLD

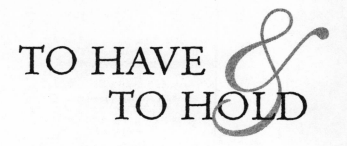

*Bible stories of love, loss
and restoration*

ANNE JORDAN HOAD

Published by
The Bible Reading Fellowship
First Floor, Elsfield Hall
15–17 Elsfield Way, Oxford OX2 8FG
ISBN 1 84101 036 7

First published 2002
1 3 5 7 9 10 8 6 4 2 0
All rights reserved

Acknowledgments
Unless otherwise stated, scripture quotations are taken from the Holy Bible, New
International Version, copyright © 1973, 1978, 1984 by International Bible Society, are
used by permission of Hodder & Stoughton Limited. All rights reserved. 'NIV' is a
registered trademark of International Bible Society. UK trademark number 1448790.

Scriptures quoted from the Good News Bible published by The Bible
Societies/HarperCollins Publishers Ltd, UK © American Bible Society 1966, 1971, 1976,
1992, used with permission.

Scriptures quoted from the New Jerusalem Bible, published and copyright © 1985 by
Darton, Longman and Todd Ltd and les Editions du Cerf, and by Doubleday, a division
of Bantam Doubleday Dell Publishing Group, Inc. Used by permission of Darton,
Longman and Todd Ltd, and Doubleday, a division of Random House, Inc.

A catalogue record for this book is available from the British Library

Printed and bound in Great Britain by
Bookmarque, Croydon

CONTENTS

CHAPTER ONE

THE FORBIDDEN GARDEN

When God created man, he made him in the likeness of God. He created them male and female; at the time they were created, he blessed them and called them 'man'.
GENESIS 5:1–2

For as in Adam all die, so in Christ all will be made alive.
1 CORINTHIANS 15:22

A WOMAN CLOTHED WITH THE SUN

In the deep darkness before time I exist in a void, a place of swirling winds. Then the light of God shines in the darkness and his loving hand creates a physical body for me. He gives me life.

As if waking from a deep sleep I open my eyes for the very first time to a world bathed in silvery moonlight. I lie still to absorb all the new sensations: the sweet-smelling turf beneath me, the cool air brushing my cheeks, the rhythm of my beating heart. I have a body. It is astonishing—to see, to smell, to hear, to feel, to touch.

With my fingers I gingerly explore this body, discovering the different sensations and the boundaries of my being. My skin is silky; soft, smooth and warm. Next, I run the palm of my hand over the grass where I lie, luxuriating in its subtle fragrance. I breathe in deeply. My hands move further, and I feel another body beside me. At first it seems to be a part of me but I am not sure so, cautiously, I nudge it. The other grunts and moves and I catch my breath. Listening intently I distinguish a difference in the rhythm of our breathing. Yes, this is another living being, like me but not me; yet I sense that we belong together. It is as if we two breathe as one. I lie still to feel the comfort of the other body touching mine. The one beside me stirs and I snuggle up closer, feeling myself complete. So I lie here and rest in the shimmering light. I watch the clouds skimming across the sky, sometimes hiding the moon so that dark shadows cover the earth, and when they part again I see faint stars in the black vault above. For a long time I study the sky with its ever-changing patterns. It gradually turns lighter and is no longer deep blue. Even as I watch, it grows paler still through shades of grey. Then a soft rose hue creeps across the sky. Pale light dawns across the land, bringing it to life. A bird sings, then another, and another, and soon the air is full of their noisy melody. This, then, is the dawn of my first day.

My companion begins to stir and I turn my head to watch him. His eyelids flicker and open to reveal dark brown eyes gazing into mine. Heavy with sleep, they droop shut again before abruptly opening once more, wide with surprise. I see the man and he sees me, for the first time. We stare at each other. He sits up wonderingly and stretches out a finger, carefully touching my nose, my mouth, and my eyes. He strokes my long curling hair and begins to smile. Then he speaks.

'Hello!'

It is all he says. His fingertips continue to search my face, my brow, my lips, my chin, tracing down my neck carefully, as if to be sure I am real. Then he says again, 'Hello! Where did you come from?'

Before I can answer he throws back his head and laughs. I find myself laughing too. We both laugh and laugh until the air is full of the sound, echoing from the hills around us. Then the sun breaks out from behind a cloud, to flood the world with light.

When our laughter subsides a little we look at each other with inquisitive eyes, finding ourselves to be alike, but different. Then, because it seems the thing to do, we hug each other. Somehow we know we are made for one another.

'I am Adam, formed from the dust of the ground,' he says. He does not explain what he means and I do not ask. It does not seem important.

Waving his hand to indicate our surroundings, he smiles as he continues, 'I live here in the Garden of Delight; the creation of Yahweh, my God.' He hesitates then adds, 'And your God, too. This Garden is his. It's my home and now it will be yours. It is good to have someone to share it with.'

I feel pleased with his words yet there is something I want to know, 'And am I also formed from the dust of the ground?' I ask.

'Oh no,' he chuckles. 'You're special.'

'Special?'

'Yes. You are special. But I'll tell you about that later. Come, let me show you our home. Let me show you all the wonderful things there are for us to enjoy.' He takes me by the hand and pulls me to my feet, and together we begin to explore the Garden of Delight.

'Look,' he says waving his arms around in a circle, 'we are in a valley, surrounded on every side by hills so high that their tops reach the sky. One day I should like to go for a long walk into the hills to see what is beyond, but before I do that there is much to see and much to do here in the Garden.'

He leads me up a sharp rise to where we can look down on woods and grassland stretching as far as the eye can see.

'Look,' he says again, pointing to something that sparkles below, 'we have a lake right in the middle of the Garden where four rivers rise and flow out to the surrounding land.' And raising my hand to shield my eyes against the sun, I follow his finger as he continues, 'They flow to the north, to the south, to the east and to the west, watering the ground on every side. Can you see the lake?' Then, before I can answer, he goes on breathlessly, 'What am I thinking of? You must be hungry. Come over here and I'll show you what we can eat.'

'Eat?' I ask.

'Yes, yes. Let me show you.'

Adam leads me down the grassy slope and through fields strewn with many-coloured flowers. We reach a small grove where, approaching one of the trees, he reaches up and plucks a huge yellow fruit from one of the branches. Handing it to me he says, 'Here, eat this.'

I bite deep into the yellow flesh. It is soft and juicy, filling my mouth, running down my chin and over my fingers. I take another bite, and another, until I have eaten it all. Then Adam gives me another. Together we feast on the fruit. When at last we have finished we lick our lips and sticky fingers and Adam leads me on, round the Garden, giving me different fruits, berries and herbs to try. As we go we meet the animals and birds who share the Garden with us and he tells me about others we cannot see, for many come out only at night. As we approach the lake I gasp and Adam smiles. In front of us are some of the most handsome creatures I have yet seen. Their breasts are as blue as the sky; their wings speckled black and white; their tails, green as the grass, so long that they trail along the ground behind them. They are truly elegant creatures and they even wear little black and blue crowns upon their heads. As we approach they turn to stare at us. Then one or two make a strange sound and with a great rustling they shake their tails, raising them high into huge fans covered with what look like eyes. The fans look so heavy that I think they will topple over. They are magnificent. For a while we stand in silence admiring them, before moving on towards the lake. Here, tired from all our exploring, we find a shady place to rest and on a sandy bank we fall asleep, side by side. When we wake the sun is sinking towards the horizon. I lie beside Adam in the deepening shade, and we sleep once more.

The next morning Adam tells me, 'Yahweh has created everything, for us to enjoy and to care for. Nothing is forbidden to us except the fruit of a tree here in the middle of the Garden of Delight.' He points to two trees growing on a little rocky island, some way from the shore where we lie. One has silver leaves, delicate as mist, interspersed with clusters of bright red berries. 'If we touch that tree, we shall certainly die,' he says solemnly. I am still trying to fathom these mysterious words when he points to the other tree growing at the highest point of the little island. It is a curious tree, quite different from any other that I have seen. Its trunk and branches are bent and twisted into the most intricate patterns; its leaves, golden; its berries, so white they seem to glow. It dazzles me so that I have to shade my eyes.

'And that is the Tree of Life,' Adam whispers.

'It's beautiful. But, the other tree... tell me again. Why must we not touch it?'

'It is forbidden.'

'Forbidden?'

'Yes. Yahweh said that we could eat any of the fruits of the Garden except the fruits of that tree. In the very moment we eat that fruit we shall die.' Adam's voice is husky.

'What does it mean to die?'

'I do not know. I only know it is no longer living here in the Garden. Can you imagine, Eve, no longer living here?'

I cannot understand him. Why, in this beautiful Garden, with so many wonderful gifts, should anything be forbidden? Why, having given us life here, would God take it away? I stare at the trees through my fingers, afraid yet intrigued. 'We could not touch the tree, even if we wanted to,' I say. 'There is no way to reach the island, and even supposing we could, it would be impossible to climb the hill to the tree.'

'Oh, it's easy to reach the island,' Adam boasts. 'I often swim there.'

'Swim?'

'Yes,' he says, and laughs. 'Look, I'll show you.' And he jumps up and dives into the water, his brown body flashing in the sunlight. He swims with the fish, twisting and turning in the clear water. 'Come on,' he shouts. 'It's wonderful.' I dive in after him, catching my breath at the coldness of the water. Adam comes close, catches my foot and pulls me under. I wriggle free, diving beneath him, coming up to splash him before ducking away again. We dart about like the fish, weaving in and out, surfacing now and again to draw breath. We finally leave the water to lie laughing and panting on the warm sandy shore. Adam draws with his finger on my glistening wet body. His touch makes me tremble. His voice is soft and low in my ear.

'I will tell you a story,' he murmurs as he strokes my arms. 'Before you arrived, our Creator God brought all his creatures to me. "Give them names and choose one to be your friend," he said. But in the Naming of the Animals there was not one who was my equal.' Adam looks up and studies my face.

'What happened then?' I whisper.

'He came to me again. "It is not good for you to be alone," he said. "I will make a special companion for you." And what do you think he did next?'

'I don't know,' I answer. 'Tell me.'

'Guess.'

'I can't guess,' I answer, giggling because he is tickling my cheek with his eyelashes.

Adam kisses me gently on my chin. 'He made a banquet for me, to celebrate the Naming of the Animals. I had honey from the bees, aromatic herbs, seeds, olives, grapes and other fruits…' He breaks off and begins to caress me again. I sigh with pleasure, moving closer and closer to him.

'And then?'

'And then I fell into a deep sleep.' He speaks so quietly that I have to hold my breath to catch his words. 'And while I slept, Yahweh took one of my ribs, and what do you think he did with it?'

'I can't imagine,' I murmur, not very much caring what Yahweh did with Adam's rib, as I run my hands over his strong back.

'He fashioned you, my beautiful Eve. Bone of my bone and flesh of my flesh. Didn't I tell you that you are special?' He kisses me again, caressing my body tenderly, until I am burning all over. We embrace, moving together, crying out, until in a moment we become truly one flesh. Afterwards, intertwined, we sleep.

From dawn to dusk we play here in the Garden of Delight. Every day is joyful. We watch over the plants and harvest their fruits, ensuring they have sufficient water and enough space to grow. We tend the animals given into our care, milking the goats and combing the longhaired sheep. As we learn to cultivate the Garden we grow to know and understand each other better. Our desires are met before they become conscious thoughts. We want for nothing. Often in the evenings Yahweh comes to walk in the Garden and to talk with us.

These times are the most special of all. He takes such delight in his creation, while we marvel at his amazing skill. He chuckles at our delight when, to surprise us, he turns over a stone to reveal the teeming life hidden underneath it. We have seen him stretch his hand over a rock until water gushes out and cascades over the pebbles, down into the lake below. And how he laughs—so loud it shakes the very ground where we sit. But the best times are when we just sit together watching the sunset.

And now today, I have come alone to sit once again beside the lake where the four rivers rise to flow throughout the land beyond the Garden. It is my favourite place. I come here sometimes when Adam goes walking in the hills on the far side of the Garden. As I sit here I often find myself looking at the two trees on the island. They fascinate me. They are so beautiful. I have seen the fruits on the Tree of Life, which dazzle me in the daylight and glow like lanterns in the moonlight. Looking closely now, I see that they resemble peaches. I turn my attention to the nearer tree with its clusters of small red berries. Why should they be forbidden to us? Could anything so lovely really be harmful? I watch the leaves and delicate branches dance in a sudden breeze. Would it be so hard to reach that tree? The thought troubles me. Perhaps I should go and search for Adam.

THE DRAGON

Just as I start to move, our friend the dragon joins me. I always enjoy his company. He is so wise, teaching me many things; truths that even Adam doesn't know. The dragon is also one of the loveliest of Yahweh's creatures. Adam and I both like to sit with him while the three of us watch the sun set and study the reflection of the sky on the water, sometimes silent, sometimes talking. The dragon intrigues me. His skin, made of interlocking scales, is so sleek that it glistens in the sun. His scales are arranged in red, green and yellow patterns so that he seems to change colour as he moves. Even on the hottest day, he feels cool to my touch, and his body is so supple that he can entirely change the way he looks, disguising himself in many ways. Sometimes he coils around the trunk of a tree, sometimes he slithers between crevices of the rocks, and sometimes he slips deep into the sandy soil. He is able to walk on any arrangement of his six legs, one moment standing upright and swaying like a reed in the wind, the next curving down in a graceful arch to touch the water. And in the water he can lie so still that he looks like a log floating on the surface. His favourite trick is to conceal himself and then jump out on us. He has a rattle hidden in his tail and when we can't find him he teases us by shaking it.

Once, when Adam was walking in the distant hills, I was sitting here with my friend and he said, 'I have a riddle.'

'What is it?' I asked.

'It's this: how can one person be three?'

'Tell me.'

'Yahweh is the answer. He is not one person, but three.'

'How can that be?' I asked, but the dragon smiled and did not answer. Certainly it was a mystery. I remember that when Adam returned from his walk, I asked him, 'Is Yahweh one person or three?'

'What a strange question, Eve,' Adam answered. 'He is one. How could it be otherwise?'

'The dragon told me that he is one in three persons.'

'What nonsense! Of course Yahweh is one. We see him, talk with him. The dragon is playing games with you, teasing you with a silly riddle.'

'But what does it mean?'

'I don't know. We'll have to ask him.'

After that I thought that the dragon must be wiser than us because he speaks in riddles which even Adam does not understand. And so when the dragon joins me today I am a little in awe of him.

'My friend,' I say. 'I asked Adam, and he says that Yahweh is one person, not three.'

'That's because he sees only with his eyes. There's another way of seeing,' the dragon answers. Fixing his gaze on me he comes closer, raises himself up until his mouth is level with my ear, and murmurs, 'You and Adam have an inner eye. If you learn to use it, you will know that you are as great as Yahweh. You are the only creatures made in the image of the three-in-one God.'

'You must not say such things!'

'Yes, yes, you are. You are made in his image.'

'No, you must not say such things,' I tell him, putting my hands over my ears, although I cannot say why I think he is wrong. In some way, the idea rather pleases me. Perhaps it is so. Adam told me that Yahweh wanted us to rule over every living creature. But still, I feel disturbed by the words of my beguiling friend. So I reason with him.

'It is not possible for the creature to be like the Creator.'

'Why not, if the Creator chooses it should be so? The Creator can do whatever pleases him. Don't you know that?'

Feeling foolish, I laugh. 'Let's swim to the island,' I say. 'I'll race you there!' And with this I dive into the water. He follows and easily races ahead of me. Spluttering and laughing I scramble out of the water and sit beside him on a warm rock. The cold dip has not banished my disquiet. I ponder the idea planted in my mind by the dragon, and I am troubled.

If only Adam were here, I say to myself, longing to ask him what he thinks. But he will not return from the hills until sundown and the dragon is here, smiling at me. So why do I feel somehow silly and ignorant?

The sun is very bright, the water very blue, the grass very green—and the dragon is laughing. Why do I feel so uneasy? The dragon's eyes flash strangely as he weaves himself around me. Round and round he goes until I am completely encircled and unable to move away without climbing over him. Then a stray cloud partially covers the sun, and I shiver. Laughing all the time, the dragon raises his body again until he is staring into my eyes. Hissing softly, he sways back and forth, rattling his tail. Then, his head dips, slanting sideways to hold my gaze and then turning to look at the forbidden tree, so close to us.

'Look at the red berries on the tree,' he murmurs seductively. 'See how they hang in clusters, juicy and tender, ready to pick. Why don't you try one? It's just a small mouthful? Where's the harm in that?'

The spell is broken suddenly. I exclaim, 'No, no! It is forbidden. We may eat any fruit in the Garden, except from that tree—the Tree of the Knowledge of Good and Evil. We must not even touch it.'

'Why? What do you think will happen if you do?'

'We shall die.'

'Die? What exactly is death?'

'I do not know what death is exactly. But it is not being. It is not living. Yahweh said we should die if we eat the fruit and I do not want to die. Yahweh does not want us to die. He wants us to live. That is why he told us not to touch the fruit.'

'Eve…' The dragon's voice is soft and hypnotic, like a breeze rustling through the trees. 'Eve, you will not die. Believe me. Yahweh knows that if you eat the fruit of the Tree of Knowledge you will become like him, not only made in his image, but also holy and eternal. Truly gods. Now he delights in you because, just as in your innocence you have authority over the animals, so in his knowledge he has authority over you.'

While I try to think of a reason to protest, the dragon goes on, 'You lack wisdom but Yahweh has given you a brain—the power to think and to question. It is a wonderful gift and he wants you and Adam to use it. Now you are children but he wants you to grow in wisdom and understanding, to become gods. Eve, if you are bold enough to try this fruit before Adam, you can be the one to give it to him. What a gift that would be! Eating this fruit is Yahweh's test to see if you have the courage to use the intelligence he has given you. Knowledge is power, Eve. Knowledge will open your inner eye and set you free.'

'Free from what?'

'Wouldn't you like to find out? Look how good it is. Is there any other fruit so tempting, so appetizing? Try it. Just a little. Ask yourself this: if Yahweh did not want you to eat it, why did he make it look so appetizing? Why didn't he protect it with sharp thorns? Why doesn't it grow out of reach? And if you do not eat it, Eve, Adam is sure to do so.'

The dragon's words appeal to me. So why do I feel uneasy? Perhaps it is true and Yahweh does want us to use our initiative. It would be good to have my inner eye open, to be truly wise. And it would be fun to surprise Adam. So I encourage myself to believe my friend because, after all, he has no reason to deceive me. As I wrestle with my thoughts, the dragon continues to hiss quietly in my ear. The fruit does look good—crimson, plump and glistening. Slowly, I stretch out my hand and with the tip of my finger touch one of the fruits. It feels cool and smooth and it looks luscious. My mouth waters. Gaining confidence, I caress a whole cluster of the red berries, running my fingers over them cautiously. Then, I gently clasp them... and... they fall... into my hand. I am surprised and a little alarmed. It is too easy, this first step of independence. There is no clap of thunder, no flash of lightning. All is tranquil. But now I notice the silence. The birds in the Garden have stopped singing. My friend, the dragon, has slipped away. I am alone, standing on the island, in the centre of the strangely silent Garden, the stolen fruit in my hand.

I raise one shiny red berry to my lips, lick it tentatively, and then take a tiny bite. The smooth skin suddenly bursts and sweet juice spurts into my mouth. Beneath the firm red skin there is delicious yellow flesh. I take another bite. It is really delicious, more so than any other fruit in the Garden. But then as I suck on the tender flesh I nearly choke. Coughing and spluttering, I discover a small hard stone in the centre of the berry. It grates on my teeth and I spit it out. But the taste lingers in my mouth and I cannot resist the desire to eat another of the berries, and another, and another. Reaching up into the tree I pick more, and more, gorging myself.

When I have had enough—for the moment—I gather as many of the fruits as I can carry in a large leaf and hurry to find Adam. What a game I will have with him! Now I see him, far off, returning from his walk in the hills. I race across the ground and, running up to him, I cry, 'Adam, look, look at this fruit. You must try it. It's the most delicious food I've tasted yet in the Garden.'

'Oh? What is it?'

'Just look at it. So red and shiny. It's made to fit into the mouth just like this, look!' I open my mouth and suck another red berry between my lips, drawing it into my mouth, holding the stalk between my fingers. The fruit breaks away from the stalk with a little plop. Adam comes nearer. I dangle the bunch of berries in front of his face.

'Let me see,' he says, reaching out a hand.

Quickly I pull away and run laughing behind a tree. 'If you want one, catch me!'

He laughs too and chases me. Round and round we go, darting in and out of the trees, playing hide and seek between the bushes, until I collapse, breathless and laughing, on the soft grass.

Grabbing hold of me, gasping for air, Adam cries out, 'I've got you! Now tell me. What have you been up to? I thought I knew every fruit in the Garden.' He tickles me. 'Come on, tell me. Where did you find these berries?'

'Not until you try them,' I gasp, giggling. 'Close your eyes, and open your mouth.'

'Where did you find them?'

'Open your mouth!'

He obeys. 'Wider,' I say, teasing him with one of the berries, dangling it just above his lips until he snaps at it, sucking the fruit from the stalk and rolling it around his tongue. As he takes a cautious bite the juice spurts out and runs down his beard, making me laugh even more.

'Delicious,' he says, leaning towards me, parting his lips for more. So we lie on the grass, side by side, feeding each other with the fruit until we are ready to burst. Then we lie still together, holding hands, at one with each other. That is, until Adam asks lazily, 'Eve, where does the fruit come from?'

I have been drifting into sleep and his voice jolts me awake. Startled, I find it impossible to answer him. Instinctively, I let go of his hand. Our eyes meet briefly. In that fleeting glance, I see something new in his eyes—an ambiguity. I look away, for the first time unable to hold his gaze. It is as if I am a stranger to him, as if he has seen me for the first time, but not with the wonder and delight of our first meeting. Now I see doubt in his eyes and not only doubt but also curiosity. I feel unclean. Until this moment I have relished the pleasure Adam takes in my body; the way he caresses me with his eyes; the way he fondles me, searching every nook and cranny with eager desire. My passion for him has been no less. I have delighted in seeing him aroused. But now our physical differences, such a source of adventure and ecstasy, seem unclean. I see that we are separate from each other, as different as day is from night, the sun from the moon. Suddenly, unaccountably, I feel ashamed. Ashamed of my pleasure. Ashamed of my desire. Ashamed of the fear which now accompanies my desire.

Adam looks uneasy. My naked breasts shame me and I try to hide them behind my hands. My cheeks feel hot. Mortified, I avert my eyes and hang my head. The space between us is no longer a place of joyful harmony but a chasm. I find the silence unbearable.

'You are naked.' My voice sounds too loud.

'So are you.'

As if in a dream I hear Adam's suppressed, gasping breath; I hear the wind blowing too noisily in the treetops; I hear the pounding of my own heart. What have we done?

'Eve.' Adam's voice sounds harsh. 'Did the fruit come from the forbidden tree?'

'Forbidden?' I croak.

'You have picked the fruit of the Tree of the Knowledge of Good and Evil, which Yahweh said we must not touch.' He is accusing me.

'You ate it too!'

'I didn't know where it came from.'

'You didn't ask!'

'I did ask!'

'You didn't want to know. It must have been obvious where the fruit came from!' I feel my eyes smarting, a tightness in my throat.

'You knew it was forbidden. I never thought you would touch it. How could you?'

'It was the dragon's idea. He said the fruit was good. And he was right. It is good fruit.'

'It is forbidden.'

'Why? Why is it forbidden? The dragon said Yahweh only forbade it as a test, to see if we were wise enough to choose it. Yahweh made us different, making us higher than the rest of creation, giving us brains to think. He wants us to use our brains—that's what the dragon said. I believed him. And, anyway, we have not died, have we?'

Adam does not answer.

If this is what the dragon meant by having wisdom, having my inner eye opened, I don't think I like it. But I am not sorry. I am angry. It is not my fault I ate the fruit. It's not my fault Adam ate it. Why is he blaming me? I don't know what to do, so I start to run away from him, as fast as I can, looking for somewhere to hide.

THE MAN

'Come back here!' I shout but she has gone, darting through the thicket like a deer. Eve is running away from me. I cannot believe it. I am trembling all over, my hands clenched into a fist. If she had not run away I think I would have hit her. But no, that's impossible! How could I even think so? Yet I am angry—angry and bewildered. When the sun rose this morning there was not a cloud in the sky, not a question in my mind, no intimation of danger. How can things change so suddenly? I am bewildered, dismayed, and I sit down and, holding my head in my hands, try to think; but I just cry. And Eve—where is she? What is she doing? I must go and find her. She was wrong to pick the fruit, wrong to give it to me, but it is true that, knowing every tree, every bush, and every plant in the Garden, I should have guessed what it was. But I did not expect her to trick me. Neither did I expect the dragon to lead her astray. Why would he do that? Yahweh made me responsible for all the creatures in the Garden. But did he warn me not to trust them? No, he did not. Now it becomes clear to me. Of course, it is Yahweh who is responsible for all this! Now I understand, I will go and find Eve, explain it to her. I feel better already.

I jump up, and run through the Garden calling Eve. Eventually she creeps out of her hiding place and I take her into my arms and hold her tight. 'It is not your fault, Eve. You were deceived. And I was deceived. When Yahweh put me in charge of the Garden he did not warn me that some of the animals were not to be trusted. He should have warned me about the dragon so that I could have warned you.'

'So you don't think it was so bad that I took the forbidden fruit?'

'No. It was not so bad, Eve,' I say, although I feel uneasy. While it is true that Yahweh did not warn me about the dragon, he did warn me not to touch the fruit. I feel so uneasy that I draw Eve closer to me, taking comfort from the way her body begins to yield to mine. But, I notice a new hesitation in her response.

'What is it?' I murmur. 'What's wrong?'

'We are naked, Adam.'

'Of course we are!' I am bewildered.

'But—supposing Yahweh should come. We will be naked in his presence.'

'We have always been so.' I feel perplexed but it's true; for the first time I too am ashamed to meet Yahweh, naked as I am.

Pulling away from me Eve runs over to a fig tree, 'Look, Adam,' she says, 'we can take leaves from this and make coverings for the lower part of our bodies.' She knots together bunches of the leaves with long stems of grass.

Suddenly it seems like one of our old games and I laugh, copying her and picking handfuls of leaves. Then, admiring our newfound skills, we make wreaths to crown our heads, and garlands of flowers to hang around our necks.

I am so absorbed in our activities that I do not hear the sound of footsteps in the Garden.

'Listen,' Eve's voice is shrill with alarm. 'I can hear Yahweh coming.' I listen intently. Without a word I grab her hand and we run to hide.

THE PENALTY

The sun drops lower in the sky as Adam and I creep into the thickest part of the forest and crouch low in the bushes. We hear the voice of Yahweh, gentle as the breeze across the water, 'Adam, where are you? Eve, are you there? I've come to enjoy the evening with you.'

Afraid to show ourselves, but even more afraid of discovery, we scramble, bashfully, from our hiding place. And we see his familiar face smiling on us. Suddenly I feel dreadfully cold and sick. His voice seems distant. What is he saying?

'Where have you been?' he asks. 'I've been calling you. I enjoy spending this time of the day with you. I love to see the sunset. It's one of my most spectacular works. Don't you think so? Look at it! The great red orb slowly sinking below the horizon. Look at the sky, changing colour. See how its glow stains the earth!' He stops and turning to look at us, frowns slightly, asking once more, 'Where were you?'

'We were hiding,' Adam replies, his hand in mine.

'Hiding?' Yahweh sounds astonished. 'From what?'

'We were ashamed,' Adam mutters. I can feel him trembling beside me.

'Ashamed? Why?'

'Ashamed because we are naked,' I blurt out, coming to Adam's aid.

There is a pause. 'Who told you that you are naked?'

Neither of us answers. Yahweh's gaze upon us is long and searching and all at once my leaf covering seems ridiculous. Nervously I clutch at Adam, but he pulls away from me. Dark clouds begin to roll across the sky. Yahweh is no longer smiling. His face is thunderous, like the clouds, and when he speaks, his voice is like the thunder.

'Have you eaten fruit from the forbidden tree?'

'Eve gave it to me,' Adam declares.

Adam is blaming me! And what have I done? I did take the fruit, but Adam had some too. He said he had forgiven me. Besides, we had such fun. Was that wrong? I am angry, but then, why did I do it, really? I can't remember any more.

Now Yahweh turns to me, and his eyes flash like lightning. I feel exposed, frightened. My cheeks burn. Struggling to breathe, I stammer, 'It was the d-dragon's idea. He, um, he s-said you didn't really, um, mean it was forbidden. He, um, he s-said you were j-just t-testing us.' My excuse sounds feeble, even to me. But it is true. I believed the dragon. 'I d-didn't think it could do any harm, just to try the fruit.' In desperation I cry out, 'The dragon persuaded me.'

The word 'forbidden' rings in my ears. What will Yahweh do to me, to Adam? Yahweh in his kindness gave us life and so much to enjoy. Surely he cannot mean to destroy us? Surely it was only a very small mistake to eat the fruit? I begin to remember the dragon's words. Why did Yahweh put the tree in the Garden if he did not mean us to eat its fruit? Surely, as the dragon said, he intended us to explore the Garden and to use the questioning minds he gave us? It could not be otherwise, could it?

This is the second absolute silence in the Garden of Delight. It is more terrible than the first silence when I took the fruit. Now the very air seems still.

Yahweh shatters the silence, his voice reverberating round the Garden. 'Where is the dragon?'

Now the dragon, my deceitful friend, appears from among the nearby trees and flashes a quick glance at me so that I know he has been watching and listening. I think he is actually smiling.

'Did someone call me?' he asks with a defiant tilt of his head.

'Where have you come from?' Yahweh asks him.

'From roaming through the earth and going to and fro in it, as you yourself know.' I can hardly believe my ears. Who is this who dares to speak in such a way to Yahweh, the Creator?

'Yes, I do know you. I know you have set yourself against me from the beginning of time. Now you have chosen to wage war against me by deceiving this woman. Because you have done this you will be cursed more than any living creature! From now on you will crawl on the ground like a worm, eating only dust; and you will have no peace for as long as you live. You have declared war on humankind and you will never again enjoy their company. From now on you will be bitter enemies.'

I am weak with relief. Yahweh does understand who is really to blame. He sees that I am innocent, that I was led astray through ignorance, that I meant no harm.

But now Yahweh turns back to me. 'I will greatly increase your pains in childbearing. Your longing will be for your husband, but you will be subject to him.'

These dreadful words frighten me so much that I hardly notice Yahweh turn his attention to Adam. 'Because you listened to your wife, and ate the fruit, the ground will be cursed, producing thorns and thistles. Your food, which until now you gathered freely, you will in future earn by sweat and toil.' His eyes scanning our faces, he says, 'I made you as man and woman. You were the most cherished of all my creation, my crowning achievement, but you cannot be trusted.'

For the third time there is absolute silence in the Garden of Delight, more terrible than ever.

Then I hear a strangled sound—Yahweh is weeping!

No one moves. No one speaks. Eventually, Yahweh, still weeping, commands Adam to fetch two young calves. Then, taking a sharp stone he tells Adam to watch while he cuts their throats. 'See how I have to destroy these beautiful creatures of mine so that you and your wife can be clothed.' And weeping all the while he shows Adam how to skin the animals and instructs him on how the skins should be prepared as coverings—but there is no time now, we must wear them as they are, wet with blood. I shudder.

In great distress Yahweh now gathers a bundle of nuts and fruits, thrusts them into our hands and says, 'Now, go! Leave this place! I cannot trust you not to steal the fruit of the Tree of Life. Go! You will no longer walk in my Garden.'

He turns his back and slowly walks away from us.

ADAM SWEATS

The air turns bitterly cold as Yahweh goes. Night falls rapidly but neither moon nor stars appear in the sky. The earth begins to shake; I hear a deep rumbling and cracks begin to open in the ground. From the distant hills there is a roaring and flames. The hills are on fire! Terrified, Eve and I grab hold of each other and begin to run, fleeing from the Garden of Delight. The blazing hills begin to turn the sky red. Our flight takes us up and out of our valley until we reach a high place and look back. I see streams of red, molten rock appearing, far away but fast flowing. Soon the whole world will be on fire. We are surely doomed.

We run on into the night, stumbling our way up into the hills and down into the valleys beyond, afraid to pause until finally, worn out, we have to stop. Finding shelter beneath a rocky outcrop we collapse into each other's arms, too tired to worry any longer about what might happen to us. We fall into an exhausted sleep.

I wake with a start, wondering where I am—and shudder as I remember. The sun must have risen but a grey haze hides it. Everything around me is grey; the world beyond the Garden has no colour. Then, looking more closely, I see that a fine dust covers everything and fills the sky. I even find it in my mouth, my eyes, and my hair. It covers Eve like a blanket. I stand up, searching the indistinct horizon for a way of escape. In every direction fires still smoulder, charred trees point blackened fingers to the sky. Then I see a higher range of mountains ahead of us, rising calm and quiet through the half-light. We should go that way, I think, above the tumult of the lower slopes. So I wake up Eve. Before setting off again we eat some of the fruit that Yahweh pushed into our hands before we left, but it barely satisfies our hunger and thirst. We are both downcast, feeling lost and alone, mourning the life we knew, now gone for ever. It is up to me to find a way to fend for both of us, in an unknown world, full of danger. Where shall we go? What shall we eat? Yet, though Yahweh has banished us, and despite my fears, I cannot feel that he has entirely deserted us. Deep inside me I sense his presence giving me courage to hope. For what? I do not know. Is Yahweh giving us a second chance? If so, I do not want to waste it.

The air is filled with fumes, irritating our throats, stinging our eyes. After another weary trek we reach the foothills of the mountains. We climb steadily, not looking ahead, until a sheer cliff-face blocks our path. Behind us the earth continues to grumble and tremble, less violently than before but still threatening. Retreat is impossible.

Desperately, I turn to examine the cliff-face, convinced that our only hope is to find a way up and over the mountains. After some time I discover places where we can cling on with our hands and feet and so edge our way up this mountain and on into the unknown.

'Eve,' I say, turning to where she crouches on the ground, shivering and exhausted, 'we have to climb here.'

'It's impossible.' She does not even look at me as she replies.

'We have no choice. I will show you the way.'

'I can't do it,' she complains. 'I'm too tired. Why can't we stay and shelter here?'

Exasperated, I surprise myself by shouting at her. 'We wouldn't be in this trouble if you hadn't believed the dragon! If we stay here, we shall certainly die.'

'Then let me die!' she wails. 'I don't care! I don't want to live any more.'

'You can stay here if you like but I'm going to climb. It's our only chance.'

Energized by my outburst, I turn to the cliff-face again and begin to clamber upwards. I feel invigorated. It is the first time I have felt the full heat of anger. The new strength flowing through my tired body astonishes me. For a moment I do not care whether Eve chooses to follow me or not. But I have not gone far before I hear her scrambling up after me. She is calling, 'Wait, Adam. Wait for me. Don't go so fast.'

In the midst of my efforts, I feel a certain glow of satisfaction. I sense I have won a battle. It is curious—I have never felt myself to be in competition with her before.

The climb is even more difficult than I feared. Every now and then I grasp a clump of coarse grass, or an outcrop of rock, only to have it give way in my hand. I pant for breath. The air is freezing but despite the cold my body sweats profusely. Tormented with anxiety I am driven on and on, up and up, over the jagged rocks. I lead the way and little by little we ascend until we finally reach the cliff-top. We are on a small plateau; beyond the ground rises steeply again. Here we pause briefly to rest and to eat the last of our fruit. It is no longer fresh but we are so hungry that it tastes very good. Feeling a little refreshed we go on again; traversing a narrow ledge that skirts the mountain, and then climbing once more. As we struggle on I think about the change in my life because I ate the forbidden fruit. I had lived for the present moment, without a care, enjoying the pleasures of the Garden. Now each moment is full of uncertainty, fear and, worst of all, I feel fury against the woman. If she had not tricked me into eating the fruit I would not be suffering now. She is struggling to keep up with me, and I force myself to climb faster, to outstrip her, to leave her behind. Perhaps she will slip and fall and I shall be rid of her. Good. But no sooner do I think it than I am full of remorse. Supposing she did fall—how would I live without her now? I cannot imagine being alone again.

But the truth is I am alone. Eve is with me but I feel responsible for her, as if she were a heavy stone around my neck. I must get both of us safely over these mountains. If only I weren't so tired! I wonder how Eve feels. It's hard for me, but it is worse for her. I haven't got the strength to call to her, even though I can hear her below me, muttering complaints and grunting with the effort. Buffeted by the wind, on and on I clamber, over the rugged ground, barely noticing the rocks gash my feet. Every now and then I look up, straining to see how far it is to the top of this cliff. Then, reaching it, I see yet another craggy peak rising ahead and I begin to lose heart; far into the distance all I can see is mountainous terrain. Just below me Eve is clinging like a limpet to the mountainside. She looks so small. A wave of panic grips me. Closing my eyes I hang on to a rocky prominence and cry out, my voice rolling round the mountains.

'Oh Yahweh, my God. I have sinned. Have pity. Help me!'

My cry echoes and re-echoes in the vast emptiness. I am desolate. Yahweh, my true friend has forsaken me. But no, I cannot believe it, filling my lungs I shout even louder, 'Yahweh, have mercy on us. Deliver us!'

Then, with a rush of air, a dark shadow rises from the rocks above me, huge wings flapping. A magnificent bird soars into the air, screeching with annoyance at having been disturbed. I edge my way upwards and, feeling with my fingertips to see where the bird came from, I discover a hidden cleft in the mountainside. I lever myself up until, on all fours, I scramble on to a ledge, and see the bird's nest—containing a clutch of eggs. Food!

'Eve,' I call, 'come on. I've found something for us to eat.'

But where is she? Cautiously I peer over the edge and, seeing her just below, I stretch out a hand to help her up. There is just room for us to lie side by side near the nest. I give her an egg, take one myself, and we crack them open and suck out the contents. We continue until the nest is empty, then Eve starts to cry.

'The bird,' she sobs, 'the poor bird. We've stolen its young.'

Her grief reminds me of Yahweh, showing me how to kill and skin the calves to clothe us, and weeping. Choking with remorse I say, 'We have to eat.'

'Yes.' Her voice is empty of emotion but her cheeks are wet, her lips quiver. 'Oh, Adam!' Arms outstretched she leans towards me; we embrace, seeking to comfort each other. Eventually we fall asleep.

Waking very early the next morning I feel better, though I ache from the previous day's journey. The haze of dust is lifting, and I can glimpse the sun. Beside me, Eve rubs her eyes and, wincing a little, stretches. I watch her, thinking again how lovely she is, grateful to have her companionship. I hug her tight and then, taking each other by the hand once more, we set off on our journey together. All day we stumble along, mostly silent, yet closer to one another than we have been since the moment that Yahweh banished us.

The sun is high when we clamber, hot and thirsty, over some loose rocks and, tearing our way through thick scrub, see a huge gap between the mountains. Reaching it, we can see a possible way down, steeply inclined, between the cliffs. As we descend, our way twists and turns until, rounding a rock, we see the land open up below us. We are on the edge of a deep ravine, not so very different from the valley of the Garden where we lived, but barren in comparison.

'We've done it, Eve. Look!'

She says nothing but smiles faintly before sinking down to lie full length on her back, arms flung across her face, eyes closed. I collapse with relief beside her.

I wake suddenly. The sky above me is not so grey; the blue is slowly emerging from the fog of ash. The air is fresher. Eve is still sleeping so I scramble over a small rise to have a closer look at the land below us. Through the haze, I can see in the distance, lush green vegetation, and a glint of water. A river. I sit down to survey the valley below; it is not like the Garden of Delight where four rivers flow, but it is green, there is water; it gives me hope. For the first time since we ate the forbidden fruit I feel a measure of peace. And I begin to remember how we lived in comfort and ease, how we walked and talked with God in his Garden, as friends. Gone, all gone. For ever.

Yes, the dragon was wicked to tempt Eve, and she was wrong to eat the fruit. She was wrong to give it to me but, reluctantly, I now confront my own weakness. I knew it was wrong. Ever since it happened I've blamed Eve for our banishment, almost hating her. But during our arduous journey the anger has drained out of me. Now I am too tired to hate and I understand now that I was as responsible as Eve for our downfall. We both did wrong. Behind me Eve cries out suddenly. I return to where she is sitting, looking around anxiously. I sit beside her and put my arm round her.

'Adam, I couldn't see you. I thought you had left me.'

'I will never leave you.'

'I have been dreaming,' she says, 'of the time before I took the forbidden fruit and gave it to you to eat. The time when we lived so happily in the Garden of Delight. Now we have no home. All because I allowed myself to be seduced by the dragon.' Her eyes are red, her cheeks wet with tears. 'Adam, I am sorry. Can you ever forgive me?'

I tighten my hold on Eve, stroking her hair.

'You are my wife. You are bone of my bones. We are one flesh. Didn't I eat the fruit? Aren't I as guilty as you?' I kiss her forehead. 'Look, we're here. I have seen a green valley below us, and a river. We have lost our home but we can build another. Yahweh hasn't destroyed us; we have a second chance. Whatever difficulties may lie ahead, he has shown us mercy in bringing us this far; we can trust him. But remember his last words; to stay alive will be a constant struggle. Because of us the ground is cursed, producing thorns and weeds; we must work for food and discover what plants we can grow to eat. It's our punishment, Eve, but it is our life. And we share it together.'

But I am mistaken. When the time comes I am helpless and Yahweh's words come true. Eve goes through agony, labouring day and night, until with an ear-splitting scream, she gives birth. I take our infant son into my arms. A new life! So much joy, so much wonder, from so much pain.

PRAYER

Three-in-One, Creator God,
Thank you for the gift of life.
Thank you for the gift of love.
Thank you for second chances.

As our past affects our present
So today will affect all our tomorrows.
May we live well today
And so have nothing to regret.
Amen

CHAPTER TWO

THE PRINCESS AND THE HEBREW

We will never find a better man than Joseph, a man who has God's spirit in him… The king… gave Joseph the Egyptian name Zaphenath-Paneah, and he gave him a wife, Asenath, the daughter of Potiphera, a priest in the city of Heliopolis.

GENESIS 41:38, 45 (GNB)

Come, and I will show you the bride, the wife of the Lamb… He showed me Jerusalem, the Holy City, coming down out of heaven from God… On the gates were written the names of the twelve tribes of the people of Israel.

REVELATION 21:9, 10, 12 (GNB)

PROLOGUE

Eyaseyab is very old now. Her skin is winkled and cracked like old leather and so taut on her face that she has the look of a skeleton. Her hands, clutching a cup of wine, are hooked like claws. When she stands she is bent double like a bow, though her eye is as sharp as an archer's and her mind as keen as a new arrow tip.

She is not standing now but sitting, hunched on the dais at the far end of the banqueting hall. It is the privileged place, set apart for honoured servants. Beside her sits the noble Hemaka, her friend and colleague, the man appointed by the God-King, Ruler of the Two Lands, the Upper and Lower Nile, to be in charge of the household of the Lord Zaphenath-Paneah, Vizier of Egypt. And also, appointed to be the eyes and ears of the Great Pharaoh in his master's house, for nothing can happen in all the land which does not reach the ear of the Pharaoh, and there is no place in the kingdom where his enemies might hide.

The Pharaoh trusts no one. While it is true that the Great Pharaoh himself appointed the Lord Zaphenath-Paneah, yet even he must be watched. Such is the intrigue in the kingdom that the greater the authority given to any official, the more assiduously he must be spied upon. So it is that for many years Eyaseyab has kept the noble Hemaka informed of the most private happenings in the vizier's palace. The noble Hemaka and the slave Eyaseyab have a deep understanding and respect for each other.

From her elevated position on the dais Eyaseyab has a clear view of all that is taking place in the hall. She observes the proceedings keenly, nothing escaping her attention. A tribe of bearded and dusty shepherds is seated here in the banqueting hall, honoured guests of the Lady Asenath and the Lord Zaphenath-Paneah. It is inconceivable! With wondering eyes Eyaseyab watches her lady graciously entertaining these uncouth ruffians from the north, come to buy supplies from the well-stocked granaries of Egypt. Well-stocked because of the wisdom of the Lord Zaphenath-Paneah who, it is said, communes with a strange god in his dreams. Certainly the High Lord has the spirit of divination; how else could he have known about the famine before it happened? And it was certainly magic that brought him to his present exalted position in Egypt, second in authority only to the Good and Great God-King, the Pharaoh, Ruler of the Two Lands. Though it is many years since this extraordinary event took place, it is still spoken of in hushed tones in the market-places. Eyaseyab, draining the last dregs from her cup, marvels even now at all that followed, and not least at the transformation in her lady.

Who would have thought it? Eyaseyab's wilful, fastidious mistress, receiving such strangers into her own home. Recent events have so excited the old servant that she is wearied now. Her eyes grow heavy with sleep. As she nods off she thinks she hears again the voice of her young mistress, many years ago, raised in shrill dispute...

PHARAOH HAS SPOKEN

Angry voices echo from the inner chamber and I, Eyaseyab, with the other servants of the Lady Asenath, tremble. Whatever the cause of her fury, we will surely suffer for it. Rarely does she raise her voice in the presence of her father, the Lord Potiphera, prince and priest. Her rage must be very great.

Pretending to be busy about my duties as the slave given charge of those who serve the princess, I listen intently. I hope for some clue that will guide me in the discussion which I know must eventually follow. I am privileged to have the ear of my mistress, since I have served her from girlhood—and her mother before her. She will certainly report to me all that has occurred. She will ask for my opinion about her father's decree, whatever it may be, and I must be sure to speak only those words that my Lady Asenath wants to hear. At the same time I must be sure to speak words that, upon reaching the ear of the Prince Potiphera and also the ear of the Ruler of the Two Lands, as they must surely do, will not cause offence. Nothing spoken in secret remains untold. The priest's palace, like all the land of Egypt, is full of sedition.

Prince Potiphera, though not close family of the great Pharaoh, is still a blood relative and has the power of life and death over his servants. He can be unpredictable and brutally cruel. I have lived long in this house because I have learnt to be circumspect, wise as a serpent and harmless as a dove. It is a wise servant who learns to speak only words that are expedient. As I attempt to listen without listening, my lady's words are suddenly as clear as temple chimes. She shrieks, 'Marry him! Marry a Hebrew? Never! What do we know of him? Who is he? A slave. Do you know where the Pharaoh found him? In prison. And for what crime? For forcing himself on his master's wife. You cannot want me to marry such a man!'

I hear her father answer, 'It is said he was falsely accused.'

'Oh yes. Now they say he was falsely accused. Now that he has the ear of the God-King. Now that he has persuaded the Ruler of the Two Lands of his powers of divination. Now that he is thought to have the ear of a god more powerful than any in Egypt. But how do you know, father? How can you ask me to make such a sacrifice?'

Fascinated as I am by this intriguing news, I shudder. Moving closer to the doorway, I strain my ears to hear everything. The voice of the prince-priest is now resolute—and furious.

'The sacrifice, if there is one, is his. The man wears the Royal Seal of the Pharaoh, the ring which the Ruler of the Two Lands placed there himself, removing it from his own divine finger. Such a one is not to be despised; he is second in the land to the Pharaoh. There are many families more closely related to the God-King than ours, and many princesses who might have been chosen. The gods have chosen my house, and the honour is mine. Why should he deign to look on you, no higher than the daughter of one of the lesser priests?

'But father, a Hebrew! I have heard stories about them. They are a troublesome people, and war-like. Uncivilized. Uncultured. Ignorant. Besides, I am told that they smell. They know nothing of shaving their bodies and oiling their skin. How could I have union with such a man? It would be unbearable.'

'You will do as you are told!'

Now I hear a change in my mistress' voice as she turns to her mother for support. 'Mother, surely you will not allow this?'

'It is not in my hands, Asenath.' The voice is cold, unyielding as marble.

It is most unusual for my lady to humble herself and appeal to her mother, and this icy response is no comfort to those of us in my lady's household. Now her wishes are not only frustrated, she is also humiliated.

'Father, you cannot be in earnest.' I hear with disbelief my wilful mistress, the proud princess, pleading. She makes one last desperate appeal. 'What sort of family does he come from? Surely you cannot, in all seriousness, intend me to marry this man even though he now wears the Royal Seal? You cannot want the blood of our noble ancestors to be mixed with the blood of a slave, a convict. Such an act would for ever degrade our descendants. Father, dear Father, I cannot believe you will surrender me for political gain.'

'The Pharaoh has spoken. So it must be. Leave me.'

It hardly seems possible. The princess Asenath has been defeated. Even if the priest is not happy about the edict, which I suspect, when the Pharaoh has spoken, no one dare defy his wishes. Related or not, to disobey the God-King, Ruler of the Upper and Lower Nile is to risk not only death but also to forfeit a place in the Book of Life and the comforts to be expected in the afterlife. No one would hazard such dishonour. I decide to make myself scarce.

My lady will be angry that I am not there as soon as she wants me but to remain is to invite a beating. Let the under-slaves take it; I am too old to receive her lashes. Besides, I have had more than my fair share over the years, and I have other duties to attend to in the house. The worst of her fury will have abated by the time I return. She will be angry with me but ready to talk, to ask my opinion. And what am I to say? My Lady Asenath, proud, beautiful and chantress leader of the temple musicians, married to a Hebrew slave. I can hardly credit it! I will seek out my friend, the noble Hemaka. He will know what it is all about. But first I will remove the best ornaments, for it is certain that my lady will vent her rage on the furnishings as well as the servants. My lady in one of her rages is wondrous to behold. But not for me. Not today. I'm getting too old.

Eyaseyab stirs in her sleep. Her eyelids flutter and her bony fingers twitch on the empty cup. The noble Hemaka, watching her, smiles to himself and leans across to remove the cup from her hand before it falls to the ground. Eyaseyab's mouth drops open slightly as she dreams on…

DAUGHTER OF THE PRIEST

The day arrives when my lady, the Princess Asenath, is to meet her future husband. It is my job to marshal the slaves who are to prepare her for the occasion. I see that my lady is resigned to her fate and she sullenly submits to the rituals required for ceremonial dress. Preparations begin the moment that the light of the sun god, Re, reborn each morning, begins to creep over the horizon. Re will soar high overhead, his life half lived, before my lady is ready. By the end of his day, my lady's betrothal will be agreed. I wake her with a cup of fresh herbal juices before summoning the slave. First she is bathed by the women of the bedchamber who then anoint her from head to toe with the finest ointments from Arabia. When she is comfortably wrapped in a linen shawl I summon the keeper of the cosmetic box, who takes pains to paint my lady's face, carefully highlighting her high cheek bones and masking the pit-marks left on her face by a dreadful childhood illness. Above all, she accentuates my lady's beautiful eyes, with thick black kohl. Finally, the Princess Asenath is dressed in the best Egyptian linen and then the keeper of the wardrobe is called. The preparations are only half finished but, worn out by my lady's disagreeable mood, I am already exhausted.

We pause in our activities to take a small meal of honey cakes, barley beer and dates. Then the robes, heavy with elaborate beadwork and embroidery, are brought forward. They illustrate the family history and I am pleased to see the delight on my lady's face. She is proud of her heritage and now she begins to enjoy all the pampering. Next comes the keeper of the jewels, preceded by two eunuchs, bearing between them a carved wooden chest. This they set down before the keeper, who opens it reverently. Though I am well acquainted with the family jewels, I never tire of seeing them sparkle and dance in the sunlight. The keeper lifts the heavy gold collar, inlaid with precious jewels, and places it carefully around my lady's neck; on top of this collar comes the *menat*, a many-stringed necklace of heavy stone beads, symbolizing my lady's position as mistress of the music in the temple of Hathor.

My mistress shows no sign of feeling the weight she now bears. I think to myself how this it is symbolic of the heavier weight of responsibility she will carry in her betrothal. I do not envy the burden of duty laid on her shoulders by this politically expedient marriage. She is a princess with all the privileges of her rank, but I would not wish to change places with her now. Even I, of lowly birth, would not be seen in the company of a Hebrew. But to marry one! It is well known that they do not shave their skin like civilized men, they have loud voices and filthy table manners. My flesh creeps at the mere mention of their presence in the city, and my heart goes out in sympathy to my young mistress, for despite all the abuse I have endured over the years, I love her. Life in her service is the only life I know. I muse over these things as I stand back to observe my lady. I am well pleased with our efforts. Though she is still angry, she is haughty and composed. The Princess Asenath is ready.

I watch my lady's graceful form cross the marble floor towards the Grand Chamber, her soft leather slippers making no sound. She pauses briefly to glance through the lattice screen hoping, I know, to catch a glimpse of her future husband so that she can be prepared before she has to greet him. But the figure of her father, resplendent in his finest robes, masks her view. Her mother, beautifully groomed as always, reclines upon a low sofa with her ladies in attendance. One of them carefully selects grapes from a bowl situated on a bronze table, places them on a golden dish and kneels to offer them to her mistress. My lady's mother accepts the grapes, looking bored, and nibbles them. My Lord Potiphera, his senior adviser, and the keeper of the law are in quiet conversation with two or three other fine-looking Egyptian noblemen as they stand together, sipping wine. My good friend, the noble Hemaka, stands unobtrusive but alert behind the loyal keeper of the records who sits in his usual place, ready with his writing materials. Musicians play softly in an alcove. There is no sign of the Hebrew and, despite my earlier misgivings, I sense favourable omens.

The discreet rattle of the *menat*, the delicate jingle of gold bangles, and the heavy scent of musk proclaim my lady's coming. She moves across the marble floor towards her father, head high, eyes smouldering, protest in every step. Reaching her father, she motions me to bring her the musical *sistrum*, sacred token of her position as chantress in the temple. It is, I know, a final gesture of defiance. She will demonstrate to the man who worships but one god that she represents the goddess Hathor. I carry the *sistrum* as carefully as I can but I cannot prevent it from ringing slightly, sounding too loud in the stillness. I need hardly have bothered. My lady receives the instrument with a grand gesture so that it rings out noisily. I see the gleam in her eye. Her father will not have missed her meaning, but he chooses to ignore it and instead he takes her free hand, moving to present her to her betrothed, the despised Hebrew. It is then that I see, as she does, that her intended husband is the youngest of the Egyptian noblemen who sip the wine so elegantly. I gasp. I see the Princess Asenath's astonished face, the deep flush that cosmetics cannot hide. Surely there is some mistake? Surely this cannot be the Hebrew slave we have heard about? This exquisite aristocrat who bows low over my lady's hand? His fine profile suggests strength of character. His carefully draped garments reveal the physique of an athlete. When I have recovered from my surprise I glance across at my noble Hemaka. He is smiling broadly. It would appear that my lady, the Princess Asenath, servant of the goddess Hathor, has met a man well able to hold his own in the very best of company. A man who will be more than a match for her wilful nature.

Once more Eyaseyab, smiling now, stirs in her sleep. Meanwhile, the eagle-eyed Hemaka watches the proceedings in the hall with scrupulous attention.

THE VISIT OF THE SHEPHERDS

Hemaka, watching the proceedings, is absorbed in thought. Although devoted to his master, the Lord Zaphenath-Paneah, he never ceases to be surprised by his behaviour. Hemaka, the eyes and ears of the God-King, Ruler of the Two Lands, is sometimes torn by divided loyalties. To keep the Pharaoh informed is necessary; failing in this is to risk imprisonment, perhaps execution. But how to relate the present events? That is the dilemma.

These Hebrews, shepherds, first came to Egypt many months before, arriving, like so many others in these years of famine, to purchase corn. To his surprise, Hemaka noticed that his master, the Lord Zaphenath-Paneah, chose to speak to them through an interpreter. Why was that? It was not that his master, through many years of living in Egypt and adopting Egyptian customs, had forgotten his native tongue. Indeed, he was teaching his two young sons the language of the Hebrews, and every day would set aside some time to instruct his sons in the history of his people and of the One God. A God unknown in all the land of Egypt. A God who does not live in temples made by man. Hemaka, the diplomat, had become skilled in relating these facts to the Pharaoh in such a way as to ensure that no threat would be implied to the authority of the Great and Good God-King.

Why then, Hemaka mused, when these strangers came from his own land, was his master so cool towards them? Why not greet them warmly? Why treat them with suspicion and accuse them of being spies? Surely he must have rejoiced to see his countrymen and to hear his native tongue spoken once more? Could it be that his way of life in Egypt, so superior, so civilized, has made him ashamed of his origins? But no, for why then would he be teaching his sons so much about his own culture? Could it be something to do with the tribal feuds of the land of his birth?

The coming of the Lord Zaphenath-Paneah to the land of Egypt as a slave is shrouded in mystery. No one knows the truth of it. Indeed, so high has he risen in the land that no one dares ask about his origins. It is only necessary to know that he is a favourite of the God-King, and that his mysterious powers of divination have been given to him by the One God. The wise servant enquires no further. To do so is to risk the displeasure of the gods. Worse, it is also to risk the displeasure of the Lady Asenath. While the gods may be appeased, the Lady Asenath shows no mercy when she is roused. She punishes severely anyone who dares to raise a question about her husband. Indeed, loyal servant though he is, the noble Hemaka often smiles at the way his master has captured so completely the heart of the proud princess.

So why the interpreter? Why the reticence? Why the open hostility? Hemaka, watchful and curious, observed all that occurred. Clearly, the Lord Zaphenath-Paneah had some knowledge of these strangers. What could it be? Hemaka listened carefully to their interrogation but it told him little enough. Clearly his master was not satisfied because he had them thrown into prison. This astonished Hemaka greatly. Unlike other high officials, his master was not prone to putting men in prison. He preferred to find alternative means of correcting wrongdoers. But it was even more extraordinary when, three days later, the men were as suddenly released on the grounds that the Lord Zaphenath-Paneah had had a change of heart. The noble Hemaka was called to be a witness when his master spoke to the Hebrews,

'Do this and you will live, for I fear God: If you are honest men, let one of your brothers stay here in prison, while the rest of you go back with grain to your starving households. Then, if your words are true, prove it by returning here with your youngest brother. When I see him I will believe you and none of you will die.'

On hearing this, the strangers, far from showing gratitude, began a fierce argument among themselves and his master watched them closely, listened intently, then abruptly left the room. Hemaka, as was his duty, followed. He was astonished to find the Lord Zaphenath-Paneah, Vizier of all Egypt, second only to the Pharaoh himself, weeping. Never before had Hemaka seen such a thing. What could it mean?

Before the devoted servant could decide upon a course of action his master recovered his composure and returned to the room where the Hebrews were still gesticulating and shouting at each other. Speaking harshly his master singled out one of them, had him put in chains and ordered grain to be given to the others. At this they were subdued to scowling hostility.

It was so impossible to understand the next occurrence that, had he not frequently wondered at his master's cunning diplomacy, Hemaka would have thought that a spirit from the land of the dead possessed the Lord Zaphenath-Paneah. He was ordered to fill each man's sack with grain and then, in secret, to place on top of the grain each man's silver. This, he perceived, must be a trick though he could not understand it since he was also instructed to provide, free of charge, ample provisions for their journey home. Hemaka was bemused. How was he to understand and report these contradictory actions to the Ruler of the Two Lands? The Lord Zaphenath-Paneah was a clever man and did nothing without good reason. What reason could he have in his dealings with these foreigners? Why had he kept one of their number as a hostage in prison? Why did he command them to return with their youngest brother? And why the tears? What could it all mean? It was very strange.

Hemaka was not to know the answers to these riddles for many days. During these days the Lord Zaphenath-Paneah was unusually morose. Then one day, the Lady Asenath came to Hemaka and stood before him, fidgeting with her robe, looking anxious.

'Hemaka, when did you notice my lord's countenance cloud over? What has happened that he has become so changed in mood?'

Hemaka, disconcerted that the princess should addresses him in this uncharacteristically restrained way, enquired, 'My Lady?'

'Hemaka, do not pretend that you have not noticed the change in my husband. His face is clouded and his manner forbidding. He has never before been so. What has happened? You are close to him all the time. Tell me.'

'I cannot say, My Lady. The days are like any other. We sit in the High

Chamber receiving petitions from many lands, including those who live in this land of Egypt. Every day is the same. Only the petitioners vary. But not so very much. All who come are hungry.'

'But, Hemaka, something must have happened. Who has my lord been speaking to? Has he spoken with strangers, or has someone known to him approached him?'

'Truly, My Lady, there has been nothing exceptional. We receive strangers of course, every day. All peoples come to us for food because my Lord Zaphenath-Paneah stored grain during the years of plenty. All who come fear my lord because it is known that through his One God he knew of the famine before it came upon us. My lord sits, wearing the ring with the royal seal on his finger, and his gold chain of office around his neck. Each day the people come to him to bargain for grain. Those who have money pay, and those who have no money exchange their cattle, or their lands, or even their freedom. They give whatever they have. All need food to keep them alive. It is as it ever was. All give thanks to their own gods that my lord heard the voice of his One God and stored up enough food for everyone.'

'Well then, if Zaphenath-Paneah my husband has no enemies among the people who come, has the Great Pharaoh, Ruler of the Two Houses, sent a message to disturb my lord?'

The Lady Asenath is deeply distressed. Never before has she so directly referred to her husband in Hemaka's presence.

'Indeed no, My Lady.'

'Think hard. There must have been something.'

And so it was that the noble Hemaka found himself relating to his mistress a brief account of the first visit of the Hebrews, prudently avoiding the questions in his own mind. Why did his master weep? Why did he return their payment? And why keep it a secret? Why give them extra provisions? Why treat them with such generosity while at the same time keeping one of them in prison as a hostage? Hemaka could not tell the Lady Asenath all these things. He did not understand his master's behaviour so he could not explain it to the princess. Above all, he could not understand why his master expected the men to return for their brother. Surely, having escaped, nothing would persuade them to return? The Lady Asenath was right, her husband was troubled, but

Hemaka could not offer any explanation or put her mind at rest.

It was Eyaseyab who later answered his questions and told him what had followed. The Lady Asenath had approached her husband on the ornate balcony where he liked to sit and watch the broad sweep of the Nile flow past their mansion; for even in times of drought the Nile flows steadily in this place. Deep in thought, he gave no sign of hearing her approach, and she found his normally mild features brooding and sullen. Her easy-going husband was uncommonly disturbed. Eyaseyab told the noble Hemaka that over the years her mistress has grown accustomed to her husband's puzzling nature. On the one hand she found him light-hearted and optimistic almost to the point of naivety, on the other he possessed such a shrewd and calculating disposition that he had been able to rise from being a slave to his present exalted position, Vizier of all Egypt.

Eyaseyab told how the Princess Asenath had come to know the exemplary character of the Lord Zaphenath-Paneah better than anyone else and marvelled that her husband had refused to become embittered by the years of injustice he had suffered. Whereas another man might have railed against the gods, this man, her husband, had turned tragedy into triumph. It was not that he had no anger but rather that he bore no grudge. Zaphenath-Paneah was a dreamer but he had an organized and pragmatic mind. Where one man would see disaster, Zaphenath-Paneah saw opportunity. Where one man would despair, Zaphenath-Paneah would hope. Where one man betrayed fear, Zaphenath-Paneah revealed courage. A man of surprises who bore no grudges. So unlike anyone she had ever met before. Her love and respect for him grew greater as the years passed but she knew nothing of the years before he came to Egypt. She knew nothing of how he came to be sold as a slave, and she never asked. She knew, without asking, that it was taboo. When her first son was born and given a Hebrew name, she tried to ask, but was silenced by the twinge of anguish on her husband's face.

Daughter of a priest, she thought the gods held no surprises for her. But when she married Zaphenath-Paneah she discovered that his One God was unlike any other. Zaphenath-Paneah believed absolutely that the purposes of the One God could not be thwarted. This God of the Hebrews did not work wantonly or irrationally, as the Egyptian gods, and

Zaphenath-Paneah believed his God had the power to ensure that good would prevail against evil.

But, as Eyaseyab later explained to the noble Hemaka, the true story of Zaphenath-Paneah and his One God was finally revealed some days later. It happened on the day that the Lady Asenath decided to accost her Lord on the private balcony he set apart as a place of prayer. It was not a temple but she knew it was hallowed ground to her husband. She knew he did not like to be disturbed when he was here, alone with his One God. But she also knew it was her best opportunity to get his attention. Seeing that he was hunched up with his head in his hands she approached cautiously, gently placing her hand on his shoulder. She felt him shudder but he did not acknowledge her.

'What is troubling you, my husband?' she asked quietly, but he did not answer. She then moved to the flagon of wine standing on a nearby table and carefully poured some into a golden goblet and offered it to her husband. Taking it absently he sipped a little, then asked severely, 'Well? You have a petition for your husband that you leave your duties to come and pour drinks as if you were my slave?'

'I have come because I know something is worrying you, My Lord.'

'What! Do you think the affairs of State are for a woman to understand?'

Asenath understood that it was not so much anger as distress that was making him behave so unreasonably. She was silent but stood her ground. Suddenly he asked, 'Where are my sons?'

'They are waiting in their chamber. They are ready for their lesson.'

JOSEPH AND HIS STORY

Eyaseyab recounted to the noble Hemaka how a brief smile then crossed the face of the Lord Zaphenath-Paneah because, a humble and honest man, he knew he was being perverse. He was grateful that his wife had, as always, anticipated his need. Spending time with his children always revived him when he was weighed down by the affairs of State.

'Have them brought to me here.'

The Princess Asenath went to the door and clapped her hands, instructing a servant to fetch the nursemaid and the two young princes.

They soon appeared, dressed in fine linen loincloths, and ran eagerly to their father. Taking their tiny hands, he placed Ephraim at his left hand and Manasseh at his right hand. Then he gazed into their smiling, up-turned faces. He seemed to make a decision and, turning to his wife, said, 'Yes. You are right. There is something I have to tell you. Come and sit here beside me.' He lifted his sons and sat them, Ephraim on his left knee and Manasseh on his right. For a long while they all sat in silence—even the children—waiting.

'My name is Joseph. I am the son of Rachel and Jacob.' Then, his voice gruff with emotion, he continued, 'I have eleven brothers. And I have spoken to them, here in the land of Egypt. They came to buy grain.' He said again, 'My mother Rachel called me Joseph.'

The children fidgeted and their father gently lowered them to sit on the floor at his feet. The little princes, seeing the solemn look on their mother's face, and sensing the importance of the occasion, sat gazing up at their father. Asenath sat very upright, very still, her eyes on her husband, her hands clasped tightly in her lap.

And Joseph, the Lord Zaphenath-Paneah, Vizier of the Upper and Lower Niles, he who has the ear of the God-King, Ruler of the Two Lands, wept. And the Princess Asenath, chantress of the temple of Hathor in Heliopolis, held him in her arms. And the young princes watched and wondered. And, behind the ornate doors, the nursemaid and Eyaseyab also watched and wondered.

And so it was that Joseph told his wife and children the story of his home in the land of his birth. He spoke of his mother, Rachel, so beloved of his father. He told how his father had laboured in service for fourteen years for her because he did not have the price of a dowry.

And Eyaseyab, almost beside herself with excitement, told it all to the noble Hemaka, he who is the eyes and ears of the Pharaoh. How, as a child, the Lord Zaphenath-Paneah, called Joseph, had dreamed dreams. In his dreams he saw the sun and the moon bowing down to him. His father had been angry, his brothers jealous. In a fit of rage they had set upon him, thrown him into a pit and left him to die. Relenting of their evil, they had sold him to slave-traders instead. Then, serving in the house of Potiphar the captain of the guard, he had been seduced by Potiphar's wife. Though he had fled from her, yet still she accused him and had him thrown into the dungeon. His One God had brought him out and given him favour in the eyes of the Pharaoh.

'And then, my dear, Pharaoh commanded you to marry me.'

'I'm glad he did,' my lady replied.

All these things Eyaseyab gleefully recounted to the noble Hemaka.

EPILOGUE

Observing the scene now before him in the banqueting hall, the noble Hemaka recollected that life had continued much as before, but the love binding Joseph and Asenath had grown deeper and stronger. For another year the severe famine continued. The people of Egypt grew thin. Starving foreigners came from far and near to buy the corn which Joseph had stored during the years of plenty when the god of the Nile was favourable with the floods. But Joseph's brothers did not return, though he longed for them.

But then there came a day when a messenger arrived to say that the watchman had seen the men of Canaan returning. A great feast was prepared, the very feast which finds Eyaseyab asleep on the dais at the far end of the banqueting hall. The feast which causes the noble Hemaka to be deep in thoughtful observation. The Lord Zaphenath-Paneah has a plan but he has not yet divulged it to his servant though, watching the Lady Asenath as she smiles at her husband, he feels sure she has had some part in it.

The noble Hemaka marvels. Watching the man born as Joseph to a Hebrew woman, who has risen to be second only to the God-King, Ruler of the Two Lands, he thinks it is a story to match any tale of the gods of Egypt. Here is his master who walks so close to his Hebrew God. Here is the Lady Asenath with the young princes Manasseh and Ephraim. And here are the unshaven men, shepherds and nomads, who barely knew how to use the bathing facilities made available to them, all seated together here in the palace, and all kinsmen to Joseph, the Lord Zaphenath-Paneah.

The noble Hemaka, wise and devoted servant, has yet to find words to explain to the God-King, Ruler of the Two Lands, all that has happened to his vizier. The noble Hemaka watches and wonders. And asks himself, who is this strange One God of the Hebrews? A God who takes such a vital interest in the affairs of his people? And, what will be the outcome of this extraordinary feast? What a story he will have to make his name live when he tells it to the writer of the records!

PRAYER

Creator God,
help us to face our prejudices,
to listen to those who are different from us
and to learn from them.
We thank you that friendship and intimacy
take time to grow.
May we, by patient endeavour,
grow into that enduring love,
such as you have for us.
Amen

CHAPTER THREE

THE GRIEVING PARENTS

Samson… said to his father and mother, 'I have seen a Philistine woman in Timnah; now get her for me as my wife.' His father and mother replied, 'Isn't there an acceptable woman among your relatives or among all our people? Must you go to the uncircumcised Philistines to get a wife?' But Samson said to his father, 'Get her for me. She's the right one for me.' (His parents did not know that this was from the Lord…)

JUDGES 14:2–4

Who has known the mind of the Lord? … Who has ever given to God, that God should repay him? For from him and through him and to him are all things.

ROMANS 11:34–36

PROLOGUE

One day, one dreadful day, the quiet life of my family changed, for ever. It was the beginning of the end of all our hopes. It happened like this.

Samson comes bounding up the hill towards our home, his face aglow. He bursts into the house shouting at the top of his voice, 'Mother! Oh, mother, I have met the most marvellous girl. I am going to marry her. She is so beautiful. I have never seen anyone like her. Just wait till you see her. You'll love her. She is the most marvellous girl in the land. I want you and father to get her for me. Soon! Soon! I can't wait.'

And laughing and shouting he grabs me around the waist and dances me around the room until I am dizzy.

I am Haggith, the wife of Manoah of Zorah. I will tell you my story.

THE STRANGER ON THE ROAD

The sun is setting fast as, weary from my work in the fields, and weighed down by the bundle of barley slung across my shoulder, I make my way homewards. The track is lonely and the way long. In the dim light I can barely see the track but it does not matter because I know it so well. I come this way often and am familiar with every rock, every parched shrub, and every clump of grass. My feet are covered with dust as I carefully pick my way over the rough, uneven surface, pausing for a moment to shift my load to the other shoulder then, wiping my brow, trudge on again, deep in thought.

'It was so hot today. Almost unbearable. But I worked hard in the fields and I have gathered a fine crop. Manoah will be pleased. I wonder if he has been as fortunate as I have been? It's a long time since he caught game for our pot. Never mind. We will have bread enough. Perhaps we will have eggs too because I spied a partridge's nest when I passed this morning, I will look to see if I can steal some eggs on my way home.'

I walk a little further before pausing once more to shift the position of my load. It seems to get heavier with every step.

'I must be getting old. I wish I had a daughter to help me, or even a son. A son might help me before he grew strong enough to hunt with his father. But, I have no child, and it seems I never will. It is many seasons since Manoah took me as his wife from the house of my father. The times for sowing and the times for reaping have come and gone so often since, yet I have not conceived. If it was going to happen it would have happened by now. I find it hard to accept that I am barren. It is the greatest sorrow of my life and every day I pray to the God of Israel, the God of our fathers, to give me a son. He does not answer me; but still I pray. He may yet hear me. My husband Manoah is a good man. Sometimes I am afraid he may take another wife as the Law allows, one who can give him sons to take away his shame. But no, Manoah will not divorce me. He never utters a word of reproach. He has great faith, saying that in the history of our people God has often blessed the barren woman, reminding me of Sarah, the mother of our people, who had a son late in life.'

This is how I ponder as I plod along the track.

Ah, but we are happy together, Manoah and I. Happier than most. Still, I do wish I might have been able to give him a son. Just one son. I wonder if we are being punished? Perhaps we have offended God in some way. Or perhaps we are paying the price for the sins of our fathers. It is not hard to think so because it is forty years since the death our leader, Abdon, a just man who taught us to live by the Law of Moses. Since then our people have neglected the truth and we have suffered a great deal. The Sea People, with their iron chariots, invaded our coasts and plundered our land. They are Philistines, wealthy merchants, fierce warriors who treat us with contempt. But, seduced by their profligate way of life, many of our people have learnt to live among them, intermarrying and worshipping their strange gods. Manoah and I try to live according to the God of our fathers, but it is difficult in these godless days. How can we understand all that is required? Who can teach us? Perhaps our sacrifices and prayers are not acceptable? Who can say?

All these questions trouble me as I walk along. Because I am so deep in thought I forget the heavy load on my shoulders.

'There is a remnant among our people still faithful to the God of our fathers. These continually pray for deliverance from the Philistines and, remembering how the Israelites were led out of bondage in Egypt, so they pray that God will raise up a champion to liberate his people in our day. My husband Manoah is one of these. Dear, good, Manoah. What a happy woman I am. We are comfortable together, Manoah and I.'

I find myself smiling and I quicken my step, so lost in my thoughts that I do not see or hear the stranger approaching.

'Wife of Manoah!'

'What's that? Who's there?' I exclaim and, looking up, now see the stranger, shadowy in the gathering gloom. He stands in my path, blocking my way. I gasp and drop my load in surprise and the barley scatters on the ground at my feet. To hide my consternation I stoop to gather it together, at the same time hastily rearranging my shawl over my head. To add to my discomfort and alarm the stranger starts to help me. What kind of man helps a woman, a stranger? I am wary as he binds the barley together and hands it back to me.

'Wife of Manoah,' he says again.

I am confused. No man of my tribe would address an unaccompanied woman. My instinct is to fear that he is a Philistine who may rape or murder me, and yet he shows no ill will; indeed, he has helped me to collect my barley together. And he is not dressed like a Philistine. Who is he? Why has he approached me? How does he know my name? What kind of man is he? My heart is beating fast. My breathing is quicker. There is something indefinably awesome about the stranger. I feel his piercing gaze and, not daring to meet his eyes, I murmur, 'Who are you, sir?'

'I have a message for you.'

I look up, surprised. 'A message? From whom?'

'I am the servant of Yahweh, your God. I have come with a message for you.'

'For me? What message can you have for me and not for my husband?'

'It is a message for you to share with your husband.'

Now my curiosity overcomes the last vestiges of my suspicion. 'I? I am to tell my husband the message of the Most High God?' I am incredulous. I cannot imagine the God of Moses speaking to a woman at all, let alone to one who is married and whose husband has power over her.

'The message is for you because it concerns you most of all.'

It concerns me? I say nothing. What can the stranger, the angel, have to say to me?

'I have come to give you welcome news.'

'Welcome news?' A spark of hope stirs me.

'Yes. You have been married long enough to bear children but until now you have been unable to conceive. I have come to tell you that you are to have a son.'

'A son! I am to have a son?' I gasp, drop the barley again, and once more it scatters all over the ground. Incredulous, I feel myself flush, and clasping my hands to my face almost swoon for joy. Recovering myself a little I exclaim, 'What do you mean, I am to have a son? How do you know? Who are you? Are you a prophet?' My questions tumble out. Not for a moment do I doubt the man, which is extraordinary. How can I believe a perfect stranger who meets me on the twilight road? But, strange as it is, I do. For a moment I am oblivious to the strange messenger who is even now stooping at my feet to gather together my barley all over again.

'A son!' I gasp. 'I am to have a son? I am really going to have a son? But,' I struggle to be realistic, 'but, how do you know?'

The news is so unexpected and so hard to believe that I wonder if I am dreaming. Have I been in the hot sun for too long? Then he hands the barley back to me and it is real enough. I clutch the bundle for reassurance, asking, 'How is it possible? Surely, sir, you have made a mistake? You have mistaken me for someone else? It is not Haggith, wife of Manoah, you are seeking.'

'Hasn't Haggith prayed fervently that she might conceive and bear a son?' The stranger has a smile in his voice as he answers. 'You are Haggith, are you not? I am here to tell you, you are to have a son—and no ordinary son.'

I am shaking but I listen keenly.

'He is to be a leader of his people. The child you bear will be a Nazirite, under special vows. No razor must touch his head. He has been chosen to begin to deliver Israel from the Philistines. And you yourself must observe the same disciplines as those who are set apart to serve the Lord God. You must not drink any wine or any other fermented drink. You must not eat any of the food forbidden by the Law of Moses. Nothing unclean must defile you.'

'But—but...' as I struggle to find something to say the stranger vanishes. As suddenly as he appeared, he is gone and the road is empty. The full moon now emerges from covering cloud and floods the barren terrain with its cold light. The road is straight. The ground is flat. There is nowhere for a man to hide.

Bursting with excitement I quicken my pace and hurry home to my husband. I press on as fast as I can, and when I am nearly home I shout for my husband, 'Manoah, Manoah!'

Dear Manoah is a simple man, and I know he loves me very much, as indeed I love him. One of the things I love about him is that he accepts life as it comes. I know he is sad that we have no children but he does not brood about it. It is our destiny, he says. Even if he could afford it, he has no desire to take another wife, he tells me. 'The wife I have is capable and worth more than jewels,' he adds. 'You are strong, hardworking and thrifty, but you are also generous to the poor. When I look around at my neighbours I see that many women make good wives but none can match you, Haggith.' That's what he tells me. Yes, Manoah loves me and I love him.

Sometimes I know that he looks enviously at his brothers and neighbours as their children play around them, but at other times he says, 'Look at how exhausted our friends are, losing sleep when their children are young, anxious when they are sick, and troubled when they go astray. Look at how hard they have to work with so many mouths to feed. And see how their children behave: rebellious, wilful, ungrateful, demanding. See how their mothers weep and their fathers despair. I think we have been spared a deal of trouble, Haggith.' And I know he almost believes it. 'If I am not to have an heir, so be it,' Manoah says. 'It is an evil world. Not a fit place to bring children into it.'

Yet I know that he does have confidence in the Most High God whose purposes are inexplicable. And now, I have confidence, too.

Still calling his name, I finally catch sight of him. From the weary way he is trudging home I can tell that his day has been fruitless. He left before sunrise, yet he is returning by moonlight, empty handed. He found no prey. It is many days now since he caught game for the cooking pot, it would be good to eat meat once more. But I have been to the fields, as I do every day, so there will be bread enough to eat—and, I remember, we will have the fresh eggs that I found before I met the stranger on the road.

'Manoah, Manoah!'

He is nearing the door when he hears me, near enough for me to see the surprise on his face and I know he is wondering why I am so late, so agitated. He is too far away and I cannot get my breath, so I drop my load and wave my arms. Alarmed now he drops the bundle he is carrying and runs towards me and I throw myself into his outstretched arms.

'Whatever's happened?' he exclaims.

Trying to get my breath I gasp, 'There was a man on the road...'

I am not aware of my dishevelled state, my wild eyes, my flushed cheeks, my disarrayed hair. I fail to see that my dear, uncomplicated husband is jumping to the wrong conclusion. Suspicion in his voice, he repeats, 'A man? What kind of man? What has he done to you? Haggith, why are you so upset?'

'Upset? Oh no! I'm not upset! Not at all!' I blurt out. 'I'm excited! Yes! But I am not upset! I must tell you. Manoah, I am going to have a baby. We are going to have... a son! A SON!'

'Yes, yes, my dear,' he murmurs kindly. 'Come along, now. You have been out in the sun all day. You are tired. We are both tired. Let us go home. We will eat. We will rest. And you will tell me all about it.'

He doesn't believe me! He talks to me as if I were a child. Manoah gently leads me to our house, sits me down beside the cold embers of the fire, lights the oil lamps and turns to look at me. All the time I babble on and on about the man I met who told me I would give birth to a son who would be a leader of his people. Now suddenly I am very tired. Too tired to talk. Too tired to explain. I lie down. I close my eyes.

'Haggith, wake up!' He is shaking me. I hear him saying, 'You cannot sleep now. We must talk.' Why does he sound so serious?

'I'm too tired.' I say sleepily.

'This will not wait until morning,' he says angrily, grasping my shoulders and forcing me to sit up. Why is he angry?

'We must talk about it,' he says sternly. 'It is obvious that something bad has happened to you. Tell me about the man you met. What happened?' Rubbing my eyes I cannot understand his mood.

'We will bear your shame together. I will not divorce you, but you must tell me quickly. Then,' he takes a deep breath, 'then I will go to our neighbours. Together we will find the man. We will deal with him as the law demands. We will kill him, be he ever so strong and ever so powerful a Philistine.'

The terrible truth dawns on me. Now I am wide awake. 'Oh, Manoah. No, you do not understand! No one has harmed me. No, certainly not.'

'What do you mean, woman?' He is exasperated. 'Why all the fuss if you have not been harmed?'

'Dear Manoah, I will explain. But, I should like a little water first.'

He looks at me keenly. 'Yes, you are exhausted. I will get you some wine from the jar,' he says.

'No, no, Manoah. I must not drink wine,' I tell him anxiously. 'Water, just a little water, please.'

He gives me an astonished look. 'No wine? Whyever not?'

I do not answer him but look at him, feeling desperate. Without another word he goes to fill a goblet from the water jar. He gives it to me and I drink deeply. Then, feeling refreshed, I place the goblet carefully on the floor, smooth my tunic, run my fingers through my hair and begin my story. I tell him calmly now of my meeting with the man, a messenger from God. When I have finished we sit quietly together in the light of the flickering lamps.

Eventually Manoah says, 'I will pray to the God of our fathers and ask him to give me wisdom, to open my eyes, to help me to take in all that this means. In fact, I will pray for him to send the man back again, if he was truly God's messenger.'

THE STRANGER IN THE FIELD

It is not that he does not believe me but, like me, Manoah finds it hard to believe that God should choose us to be the parents of a leader for our people. We both feel inadequate for so great a responsibility. We have no experience of caring for an ordinary child let alone one to be brought up as a Nazirite! It is an awesome obligation and it troubles both of us a good deal. It worries Manoah so much that he does not even look happy about it! In fact, the morning after telling him my momentous news, while I pretend to be asleep, he gets up very early to go to his secret place of prayer, half hoping, I know, that it is all a mistake. He will be on his knees, his arms stretched out to heaven, pouring out his heart to God.

Several days later I am in the barley field resting in the shade of a fig tree. Since I met the stranger, Manoah has risen at dawn each day to pray and offer sacrifices to the Most High God. I have been working since first light. It is noon. Eyes closed, I rest here, enjoying the gentle breeze which, fragrant with the scent of lilies, drifts over me. It is strange because there are no lilies in this part of the field. A shadow passes over the sun, disturbing me, and I open my eyes. He is here, the messenger of God.

'Oh!' I scramble to my feet. 'Stay there. Please, sir. Manoah, my husband, wants to speak to you.'

Not waiting for an answer I turn and run and run towards the house calling all the time, 'Manoah! Manoah!'

And Manoah, seeing me from where he stalks game higher up the plateau, begins to run towards me; slithering and sliding down the steep slope, stones and pebbles scattering on every side.

'What is it?' he cries as he sprints up to me.

'Come quickly!' I am out of breath. 'He has returned—the man who spoke to me—he is in the field—come and see!'

I bend over, holding my sides, trying to get my breath. Then Manoah takes me by the hand and we hurry back to the field. I hope the man is still there.

He is sitting under the fig tree where I sat. Manoah, consumed with curiosity but still suspicious, approaches the stranger, 'Are you the man who met my wife on the road?'

'I am,' the stranger replies.

Manoah looks uncertainly at him, choosing his words carefully. 'You told her she is to have a son?'

'I did,' the stranger answers, smiling.

I see a baffled look on Manoah's face. It makes me want to laugh. Then Manoah asks, with some trepidation, 'And, when the child is born, he... er... what sort of life will he have?'

Now the stranger, still smiling, answers, 'He is to be a Nazirite for the whole of his life, dedicated to God. And because of this, as I explained to your wife, she too must abstain from all that is unclean—taking no wine, no fermented drink of any kind, and living by the Law as a Nazirite herself —until he is born.'

Not daring to ask any more questions, and still only half believing his senses, Manoah invites the man to eat with us. 'I will prepare a kid from my flock for you,' Manoah says, though he knows we can scarce afford it.

'I cannot accept your food,' the man answers, 'but if you will, prepare a burnt offering to sacrifice to the Most High God.'

Manoah, still somewhat agitated, asks the man his name but he refuses to say. Manoah is taken aback, and so am I. Why should the stranger refuse to say who he is or where he is from? All the same, he has a quality about him that defies further questioning. So Manoah and I go to prepare everything the Law requires and when all is ready we go, with the stranger, to my husband's private place of prayer. Here, on a slab of rock, we sacrifice an unblemished young goat as a burnt offering with fine flour, olive oil and incense as a grain offering to honour the Most High God. The flames rise high into the sky, Manoah and I lift our hands and eyes heavenwards in worship and, even as we watch, we see the stranger ascending in the flames, with splendour, until he is lost from our sight. We fall to the ground in fear and reverence of the God of our fathers and all his angels.

THE STRANGER IN THE HOME

The years pass. We do not see him again, the messenger of God. I did indeed have a son, Samson. He was set apart from birth as we were instructed, dedicated as a Nazirite; abstaining from wine, never having his hair cut, and never going near a dead body. These signs show that he is consecrated to serve the Most High God. We were overjoyed when he was born and, after his birth, I had other children—brothers and sisters for Samson. We, who thought we would never have a family, now have many sons and many daughters and we love them all; but in particular we love our first-born, the child of promise. He is the light of our lives; in every sense a special child. Perhaps, to be honest, we are a little in awe of him, a trifle overwhelmed at the responsibility of having a child who is set apart for a special purpose. We idolize him. He can do no wrong. He is a beautiful child, perfectly formed, strong and sturdy. His crowning glory is his mass of hair which, uncut from birth, tumbles like a lion's mane down his back. Indeed, as he matures to manhood he is a lion of a man. He is the servant of God. He is our child. We are as proud of him as any parents can be.

True, he is a little wild and inclined to be wayward but he has been chosen. As his mother I find it difficult but necessary sometimes to protest at his behaviour,

'Now Samson...' I say. And he always laughs, turning his magical smile on me so that I cannot help smiling back. 'He is only a young man,' I reason, 'and he has great responsibilities ahead of him. He must be allowed to enjoy his youth.'

In this way I comfort myself when he is unruly, self-indulgent, demanding. To Manoah, Samson can do no wrong. Whenever I express my concerns he replies, 'Let the boy be, it's only natural for him to...'

His brothers and sisters know that we favour Samson. Sometimes I hear them grumbling about him together, but even they find it impossible to stay angry with him. Like everyone else they are captivated by his charm. There is something irresistibly endearing about him. He treats life as a great joke. When his younger brothers copy his daring pranks they always run into trouble, leaving Samson to laugh with glee. And, try as they might, they cannot match his hunting skills.

My daughters fall over themselves to please him. When they bake bread, Samson must try it first. They fight to serve him at table and squabble about who should mend his clothes. They bicker over him all the time and he rewards them all with his dazzling smile.

My husband and I see all this with pleasure because he is our first-born, the child of promise. Of course, Samson admires, and is admired by, many young women in the community. His sisters' friends visit us all the time and love to flirt with Samson, who makes no attempt to hide his appreciation. He loves them all. In fact, I do worry that he has a weakness for the opposite sex. Even Manoah has taken him aside on more than one occasion to warn him.

'Samson, you are a fine boy and of course you like these young women. I would be surprised if you didn't! And naturally they are all after you. But you must be careful you know. Don't lead them on, and don't be taken in by them, either. Women can get a man into a lot of trouble. Be wise, take your time, wait until you find a fine woman like your mother before you settle down.'

And Manoah tells me that Samson laughs in his merry way and tells his father not to worry.

'I am a young man,' he says to his father, 'and full of energy. Of course I enjoy the company of women. Besides, father, you cannot blame me. Why, I try to fend them off but you see how they pursue me! Is it my fault if they find me so handsome? Aren't I a fine-looking fellow? Haven't you said so yourself? Even my mother and my sisters say that they are not surprised that women chase after me. I admit I enjoy it. And you, father, wouldn't you be flattered yourself if you were me? Surely, you would! In any case, supposing I did not enjoy all the attention, what could I do? How should I keep them from fluttering their eyelids and swinging their hips at me? They are like bees in a field of lilies!'

And Samson's laugh is so infectious that his father finds it impossible not to laugh with him. And I laugh too when he tells me.

'Nevertheless, my son,' I hear Manoah say to Samson, 'listen to me. Women are like serpents. The most beautiful are the most deadly. You may think the snake is asleep when you come across it on your path, but if you touch it, it will strike. Beware my son. Listen to what I say and do not forget it.'

'Oh, come now, father,' Samson chuckles, looking towards me. 'Surely you will not call my sisters serpents? Surely my mother is no serpent?'

As always Manoah is silenced by the quick wit of our son. When he shares his nagging doubts with me I try to reassure him, not wanting to accept the evidence of my own eyes.

'But, Manoah, he is a chosen one, a Nazirite. Have you forgotten what the messenger of God said to us concerning him—that he is to lead his people, our people, to deliver us from the Philistines? The Most High God gave him life, and called us to set him apart for special service. Surely our son, the chosen one, cannot fall into temptation? Surely the Most High God will protect him? He will not desert the one he has called.'

'That's true, Haggith,' Manoah answers thoughtfully, 'and yet is it not possible that Samson may himself desert the Most High God? And I think the messenger said he would begin to deliver his people—not that he would deliver them. Sometimes I feel uneasy, Haggith. And yet, you are right, we have prayed for him, taught him the Law of Moses, and constantly offered sacrifices for him.' Then Manoah scratches his head, shrugs his shoulders and continues with his work. And so Manoah and I try to allay our anxieties about our son. I am more easily reassured than Manoah who, I can see, remains uneasy. Selecting the very finest of his kids he goes more often to the rock of sacrifice, our own holy place, to sacrifice burnt offerings for our son. He thinks I do not know. He thinks it will confirm my fears that Samson, my special son, is in error. I do know, yet I cannot face my suspicion that, contrary to his Nazirite vow, Samson secretly indulges in strong wine and in promiscuous behaviour. I comfort myself with memories of the messenger who foretold Samson's birth. Also, I do not cease from praying for my son, morning noon and night. I implore God to keep him safe and to keep him from sin. I do not tell Manoah how much I pray; we each bear the burden alone, thinking to spare the other and lacking the courage to share it.

It is impossible not to be proud of Samson. He is such a fine figure of a man. There is nothing he cannot do if he sets his mind to it, and so the secret nagging fears that both my husband and I experience are never mentioned. We are becoming strangers to each other, and our son has become a stranger in the home.

A STRANGER IN THE TOWN

Many years have passed and I stand now, quite alone, at the place where Manoah lies, in the tomb of his father and his father's fathers. With shoulders stooped and head bowed low, I stand dry-eyed, oblivious of the dry dust blowing in the wind that settles in a fine brown film on my crumpled clothes. I no longer feel the hot sun on my back. I might be just another rock, stark in the barren landscape. I am numb.

As in a half-remembered nightmare I recall that fateful day when Samson came bounding into the house, intent upon marrying the daughter of a Philistine... Yes, that was the start of it... He refused to listen to our protests. He was besotted with the girl... He must have her. He would have her. The more we protested the more obstinate he became. In a flash of blinding clarity I recall Manoah's words clearly: 'You are a Nazirite. How can you even think of marrying a foreign woman? Aren't there enough fine girls among our own people?'

But Samson refused to listen. 'She's the one I want, ' he said. 'Get her for me!'

'Yes, that was how it was,' I think. 'That was always the way with him. We could never refuse him anything. Samson wanted a woman. A Philistine woman. And what Samson wanted, Samson must have!' I am angry now. Angry with Samson. Angry with Manoah. Angry with myself.

That was how it started. All that followed is because Samson wanted a Philistine woman and Manoah could not refuse him. And that's what killed Manoah. Samson finally broke his father's heart. And Samson?

'Aah-ee, aah-ee!' I groan aloud, tearing at my clothes. 'Samson! Samson! My son, Samson.'

I can hardly bear to think of him, Samson, my precious boy, with his carefree manner, his immense strength, his beautiful bronze body, his glorious hair, a thick mane that tumbled down his back. And his eyes, his keen sparkling eyes. My Samson.

The sun burns into my back and bakes the ground at my feet. But I shiver. With a sudden movement I throw my head back and with arms outstretched to the cloudless sky I scream aloud, like an animal. The still air carries the cry to the hills and it reverberates around the valley.

I clench my hands and double up, beating my chest. I crumple and fall on my knees. I beat the ground with my fists.

'Samson, my son. Our son, born to be a leader of your people. Our beloved child. A child of promise.' I pummel the ground and groan in despair. 'Our son is in chains—Philistine chains. In a Philistine prison he turns the mill stone.' I weep. 'Where is the promise now? He is a Nazirite; they have shorn his head. They have torn his skin with their lashes, and they have...' I gasp for air. I know the truth but I cannot say it. I know... they have... gouged out... his eyes. Samson is blind.

Samson is broken and Manoah is dead. The Philistines have triumphed. Samson, the light of our lives, the one who would rescue our people from the Philistines, is grinding the corn of our enemies. Where is the Lord God's promise now?

Manoah's last words echo in my head. I see his face again now, as it was when the news came that Samson had been caught in the arms of a prostitute. Manoah clutching his chest, falling to the ground, deathly white, saying, 'What have we done? What have we done?' These were his last words. I find no comfort in them.

Inconsolable, exhausted, I continue to kneel at the burial place of my husband. Eventually, heavy with grief, I rise to make my way down the long lonely track to my home.

Nearing the village I hear a voice calling in the thin mountain air. It is the voice of a stranger bringing news to the village. At first I take no notice. I do not care. What does it matter? But, what is he saying? What is that he is saying? The voice rings out over the village, echoing up and down the valley, resonating from the surrounding hills, bursting with excitement. I catch phrases hovering in the breeze. 'The temple of Dagon, god of the Philistines, has fallen… it is utterly destroyed… smashed to the ground…'

What is this? Can it be true?

As I approach, my sore eyes see a scene of utter confusion. A commotion of people mill around in shock and surprise,

'Fallen?'

'Destroyed?'

'How?'

'What happened? Tell us, what happened?'

But some are still. They have heard the news already. They listened when the stranger first arrived, and now they see me approaching. One by one they slowly turn and look at me, nudging each other into silence. I see them. An icy finger touches me. Instinctively I know that the stranger's news concerns me in some terrible particular—and this is confirmed by the hush that falls on the crowd. I approach, slowly, steadily. The sky has grown dark. A cold wind begins to blow. A storm is coming. My steps do not falter. People move aside as I approach, come close to the stranger and stop in front of him. My voice is too loud in the silence, 'You bring news? The temple of Dagon is fallen, you say?' I look directly at him. 'Tell me how it happened.'

The man is a stranger here. He does not know me, but he senses that his news has especial significance for me. Avoiding my gaze, his eyes search the crowd, appealing for a sign. Subdued by the sombre tension in the onlookers his voice is careful when he speaks.

'It was like this,' he says, watching me. 'The temple of Dagon has fallen, and Samson with it. Samson destroyed the temple and all the leaders of the Philistines were killed, with all their guests.'

I stand very still and, feeling faint, murmur, 'Tell me how it was. Tell me *exactly* how it was.'

'It was like this,' he says again. 'The Philistine chiefs gathered together to offer a great sacrifice to Dagon. They had a lavish feast and became very drunk. Then they said, "Dagon has given us victory over our enemy, the mighty Samson. He is like an old man, blind and weak, fit only to grind corn. Let's send for him to entertain us." So they brought Samson from the prison and they taunted him and made him show off his great strength—but of course they did not remove his bronze shackles.' He pauses as I clutch my throat.

'Go on,' I insist.

'Well,' he says, 'there were thousands of them, women and children too, watching from the roof and making fun of him. Then Samson shouted out loud, "O Most High God, remember me, forgive me, give me strength once more!" Then he leant against the pillars of the temple, seeming to be tired out. But a servant who escaped told me that Samson grasped the two pillars where he rested and, crying out, "Let me die with the Philistines!" he pushed against them with all his might.' The messenger stops, a look of wonder on his face.

'Yes. Yes, and what happened then?' a voice from the crowd cries out.

'Then? Why, then the pillars buckled, and the temple rocked, and the god Dagon tumbled over, and then the whole building collapsed. Samson killed more Philistines when he died than he did when he lived! It was spectacular!'

An astonished buzz greets this news. But I turn my back on the crowd and make my way to my home.

EPILOGUE

I am Haggith, the widow of Manoah of Zorah.

They come to me and ask me why I do not weep. I cannot. My grief is beyond tears. I am all dried up inside. My sorrow is like a stone in the pit of my belly. It weighs me down and drags me into a chasm of despair. I feel nothing. Just cold. So cold.

I lie beside the fire in the home of my favourite daughter-in-law. She clasps my cold feet in her warm hands and massages them with oil. I feel the blood flowing back into them. I listen to the crackling and sizzling of the dried dung on the fire, the wind moaning through the village. I gaze into the orange and red flames of the fire. I watch the smoke rising to escape through the hole in the roof, the changing patterns of the red-hot embers. And there I see the form of a man. And it seems that he is smiling and saying to me, 'This is the beginning of the work and the rescuing of my people.' And even as I watch, he is gone.

PRAYER

Most High God,
We come to you with high hopes,
Good intentions and fervent promises.
And when we get things wrong
We find it hard to accept that we are human,
Weak and fallible.
Forgive us.
We bring you now all our hopes and aspirations,
All our relationships, on earth and in heaven.
You know our desire to love,
As you love us.
Amen

CHAPTER FOUR

A WIDOW'S CHOICE

Orpah then kissed her mother-in-law and went back to her people. But Ruth stayed with her... and said, 'Wherever you go, I shall go. Wherever you live, I shall live. Your people shall be my people, and your God will be my God. Where you die, I shall die and there I shall be buried.'

RUTH 1:14, 16–17 (NJB)

So you are no longer aliens or foreign visitors; you are fellow-citizens with the holy people of God and part of God's household.

EPHESIANS 2:19 (NJB)

TWO WIDOWS

The early morning sun has not yet warmed the hut where two women crouch, huddled together, sharing the remains of the past evening's meal.

'You look tired, mother,' the younger woman says. 'Didn't you sleep?'

'I was cold but I slept a little,' her mother-in-law answers, gazing into the concerned eyes focused on her. Enormous eyes accentuated by dark rings in the thin face. A once-beautiful face now betraying telltale signs of fatigue and malnourishment.

'I am a little tired. It's of no account. You look tired too, my dear. You should have remained with your own people,' she says with a sigh. Then adds, almost involuntarily, 'But I'm glad you didn't. I'm glad you came with me.'

'I'm glad I came, too,' Ruth answers. 'I couldn't possibly leave you. You know that.'

Ruth scrapes the dry bread round the edges of her empty bowl, raises it to her mouth and chews it slowly, savouring every crumb. She ponders their situation. It is desperate. She cannot bear to see Naomi's strength draining away, the constant concern gnawing at her spirit, diminishing her. Naomi is worn out with too much hardship, too much sorrow. Ruth leans over and grasps her mother-in-law's hand.

'Don't worry. I promised to take care of you, and I will,' she declares staunchly. 'I have a plan. It is fortunate that we have returned to your home town just now, at the beginning of harvest. First the barley will be gathered, then the wheat. Mahlon taught me your laws. He said that during the harvest season the reapers are to leave the edges of the fields for the poor and the stranger to glean. So, since I am a foreigner, I will go to the fields today to exercise my right as a stranger to pick up as much as I can. I am young and still strong. Who knows how much I may be able to gather?'

'My child, Mahlon my son was right—the law does allow you to glean at the edges of the field. But, my dear, we live in troubled times. Moses, the servant of God, gave the Law to us many years ago and not many of my people follow it now. Not many are concerned with the Holy Commandments. Everyone pleases themselves, choosing to keep the laws they favour and ignoring the rest.'

'What do you mean, mother?' Ruth asks, shocked and puzzled.

'I mean that, while the law gives you the right to glean what you may, it does not follow that you will be welcome. The reapers may resent you. You are not even a poverty-stricken Israelite. I am sorry to say that even the hungry beggars of my own people are rarely welcome to take what they can. They are too often looked upon as worthless, feckless idlers, unwilling to commit to a full day's work. I am afraid the harvesters may not be as ready to welcome you as you are to work hard.'

'Mother, I must try, otherwise what is to become of us? We are penniless. We are two widows with no friends and no relations. I know we have the land belonging to your husband but it has been neglected for too long; overgrown with thorns and thistles, it is useless to us. Even though I am strong we have no tools, no way to clear the land. We have no oxen and no asses. No sheep and no goats. We do not even have seed to sow. Apart from our wedding jewels we have sold everything because the journey from Moab has cost us all we had. We must eat. I must work. Your God has brought us to this place. He will not forsake us now.'

Naomi, close to tears, gathers her tattered robe in her hands to cover her face. 'So be it,' she whispers. 'The Lord God be with you, Ruth, and bless you.' She wishes she had as much confidence in her words as her daughter-in-law has in her own youthful strength, in the laws of Moses and in the God of her husband.

Soon after this, Ruth leaves to make her way to the village, and Naomi busies herself about the small hut which they reclaimed on their return from the plains of Moab. It stands on the edge of the overgrown fields belonging to her dead husband. Broken down and derelict, it is barely more than a heap of stones. Naomi, weak though she is, sets about tugging at some of the weeds around it, trying to clear some space where they could, perhaps, plant a small crop one day. 'We left to escape famine,' she thinks bitterly, 'and now I have returned more destitute and closer to starvation than when we left. If it were not for Ruth I would be quite alone.' And glad though she is to have Ruth, Naomi grieves for her husband, Elimelech, and her sons, Mahlon and Kilion. She grieves, too, for the grandchildren she has never had.

As she works, she cannot forget the night that has just passed. A night like every other night—cold, sleepless. All night, every night, she finds herself tossing and turning, longing for the dawn. During the day, tired as she is, she can be busy about her tasks, relieving her fears and anxieties. But always at night they return to plague her so that she has come to dread the long, dark hours.

'I cannot go on like this,' she tells herself, 'but who can help me? I cannot confide in my daughter-in-law, Ruth. She is the cause of my distress. If she had returned to her own people, as I suggested, I should not have to worry about her now.'

Ruth the Moabite, and Orpah her friend, were little more than children when secured by Naomi to be brides for her sons. Already a widow, but with considerable wealth at the time, Naomi thought these marriages would guarantee her future. The girls were strong and healthy. They would surely provide heirs for her two sons so that, when they returned to her home in Bethlehem in Judah, her husband's land and property would be safeguarded. So Naomi believed. It was not to be. She has returned destitute, and with a daughter-in-law dependent upon her.

So the anxieties go round and round her head. She cannot escape them. She longs to share her concerns with someone but, because she has been away from her home town for over ten years, she has grown apart from her neighbours. Ruth, whom she loves so much, cannot be burdened with her deep misgivings. Naomi has come to rely heavily on the young woman and to share with her the concerns, uncertainties and fears of their widowhood. But these nightmares are her own. They cannot be shared.

Naomi recalls the early days when her sons married the Moabite girls. The elder, Mahlon, married Ruth and the younger, Kilion, married Orpah. Both girls were beautiful but, though Naomi was fond of Orpah, she loved Ruth. Orpah was a dutiful wife to Naomi's son Kilion, but Ruth was devoted to Mahlon. It was Ruth who wanted to learn all she could about her husband's people and homeland. It was Ruth who hoped to return to her husband's land one day, with him and his children. It was Ruth whose love was conspicuous. A naturally vivacious girl, she possessed an unaffected charm and her love for Mahlon made her radiant. She was an excellent wife, and her devotion to Mahlon and his mother, Naomi, was gossiped about far and near. Although they were exiles in her land, she loved Elimelech's family as though they were Moabites.

Ruth was devastated when Mahlon died. So suddenly. So appallingly. So incomprehensibly. It happened one day as the two brothers were shepherding in a fertile valley some distance from their village. Raiders attacked them. The two men fought bravely to save their flocks but they were hopelessly outnumbered. Despite a fierce battle they were both killed, there in the pasture, and their animals stolen. The three women were left virtually destitute. Naomi, Orpah and Ruth were united in their grief and loss, but for Ruth the loss was like a hammer blow. All the hopes and expectations she had nurtured of one day having a new life with Mahlon in the land of his birth were destroyed at one stroke. She was utterly devastated. So it was entirely natural, when Naomi decided to return to her own land, that Ruth should choose to go with her. Not for a moment did she hesitate.

All of this, Naomi understands.

NAOMI'S NIGHTMARE

Now, as the day grows hotter, Naomi turns from the field to making their hut more habitable. While turning over all these memories in her mind, she finds a sharp stone, large enough to hold, and uses it to scrape away the weeds, which have taken hold in the cracks of the crumbling walls. Then she gathers small rocks, building them on top of one another to fill the gaps, fixing them in place with mud. Her hands become scratched and sore but ignoring the discomfort she works on until, in the full heat of the noonday sun, while Ruth works hard gathering ears of corn, Naomi has to rest. Lying on her shawl in the shelter of the hut she eventually falls into an exhausted sleep. Now Naomi's nightmare returns to haunt her. As in the long hours of the night, so now in the shimmering heat of day, her accusers come, whispering in her ear.

'Go away,' she pleads with them. 'Do not torment me.' But still they come. Her long-dead husband Elimelech comes. Her firstborn son Mahlon comes. Then her second son Kilion comes. Orpah comes. Thin women with haggard faces come. Fat women, leering and mocking her, come. Her sleep is full of faces, but the only face missing is the face of Ruth. The others, friends and strangers alike, come to torment her, pointing and whispering. They mock her, accuse her, reproach her.

'Why did you bring Ruth to this country?' They ask.

'I could not stop her,' Naomi protests.

'You did not try,' they claim.

'Yes, I did. Of course I tried.'

'No you didn't, really,' the faces say.

'But, yes. Yes, I did. Orpah returned.'

'And you were disappointed in her.'

'No, no. That's not true. I told her to go. I told her to return to her own country.'

'Her own country. Yes. Her own country. You had no right to take daughters from a foreign land to wed your sons. You had no faith. Now you are paying the penalty.'

'No, no!' Naomi wants to cover her ears, but she cannot move. She wants to wake up, but she remains trapped in her troubled dreams, plagued by agonizing questions. 'Why did my husband take us to Moab? Was the famine really so bad? Shouldn't we have remained, trusting in the God of Abraham to feed us? But didn't the God of Abraham call the patriarch to leave his own land and journey in faith to another place? Did we do wrong? Why did my husband die? And my sons? Surely my name is Mara, 'bitter', because no one has suffered as I have suffered! And why did I bring Ruth, my daughter-in-law, with me? What is there for her here, in Bethlehem, the town of my birth?'

Naomi wakes suddenly. Her head throbs and she feels sick. She rises to splash a little water from the almost empty pitcher on to her face. She must go to fetch more water. Ruth will soon be home. Doubts still flood her mind.

'Ruth is working hard, gleaning in the fields. Is it true? Could I have persuaded her to return to her own land and to her own people? Should I have tried harder? Was it selfish of me to allow her to come with me? Did I play on her gentle nature and kindness?'

She does not know the answer to her questions, yet even as she struggles with her doubts and bitterness, a change comes over her. Words learnt long ago, buried deep, now surface. She calls to mind another story of bitterness. Moses, leading his people out of Egypt to the Promised Land, reached a place where the waters were bitter. The people were furious and complaining and Moses, angry with God, cried, 'What are we to drink?' God showed him a piece of wood and Moses threw it into the water and the bitter became sweet.

Remembering the story, Naomi exclaims, 'Lord God, you who made the water sweet in the desert, hear me. Your people, the people of my land, have forsaken you. But my husband Elimelech kept the faith. And I have tried to do the same. Now I am destitute; an unhappy widow, childless and unable to provide for my daughter-in-law. Oh, Lord God, you can turn the bitter waters sweet, consider me and think of my loyal daughter-in-law. Do not hold the sins of our fathers against us but turn our sorrow into joy, I beg you.'

As she prays, Naomi rocks back and forth on her knees, beating her chest and tearing at her hair. Then, at last, she lies down and falls asleep once more. This time her sleep is untroubled and peaceful.

RUTH RETURNS FROM THE FIELDS

Naomi has just woken again and kindled the fire when Ruth appears, dirty and dishevelled, but triumphant. She carries a large bundle on her head which, with a grunt of relief, she drops noisily on the newly swept floor.

'What's this?' Naomi exclaims.

'See, mother. I told you the Lord God would be with us!'

'But, child, what have you got here?'

'Barley from my gleanings.'

'Gleanings? Where could you have gathered such a load? It's not possible to gather so much, even working from morning to evening as you have done.'

Tired as she is, Ruth's eyes sparkle in the glow of the fire.

'Mother, I ache in every limb. But it has been a wonderful day. And, look, see what I've brought you.' Here she reaches behind for her shawl. Laying it on her knees and unwrapping it carefully, she produces roasted grain, dried dates, some barley bread, and a small wineskin full of rich barley wine.

'Ruth!' Naomi is astonished. 'Where did you get all this? And whose field have you been working in that you have gathered so much? It's incredible! Tell me, where have you been working?'

'I have been working in the fields of a man named Boaz. Such a distinguished-looking man, mother. And so kind.'

'Boaz?' Naomi mused. 'Boaz. I know the name, but I'm not sure why I do. Tell me more about your day. How did you come to find yourself in his fields?'

'It was wonderful! I prayed to the Lord God for guidance and strength to glean all that I could. As soon as I reached the barley fields I saw workers making their way to the finest-looking crops, so I followed them. No one spoke to me, although I noticed some looking at me and whispering together. But they were not unfriendly so I dared to follow. I watched carefully as they began to work and then I approached the overseer.

'May I follow your servant women and glean the fields after them?' I asked him, and he gave his consent. So from early morning I followed them, picking up every single stem they missed, large and small. We were in the fields for some time when I saw the landowner arrive and greet his workers in the name of the Lord God. I was encouraged to know that he was a God-fearing man. And it was good to see how much his servants respected him, and he them. They said he was called Boaz.'

'Boaz.' Naomi repeats the name again. 'It sounds so familiar to me. I wish I could remember why. My old head is not what it was. Go on with your story. Perhaps it will come to me. Tell me more. How is it that you have gathered so much in the fields of this man? And this fine food. Where did it come from? Did you remain in the same fields all day or did you move to another place?'

'Well,' Ruth says, pausing to drink the water Naomi offers her, and smiling at the memory, 'I worked on and on. The sun was scorching my back and I felt so weary, but I dared not stop. The women binding the sheaves worked so much faster than I could and I did not want to miss anything. Eventually, when they stopped for refreshment near the middle of the day, I was able to find a shady place to sit and rest. I was mopping my brow when I looked up and saw the landowner looking at me and talking to his overseer. Then the overseer came over to me, saying that his master wanted to speak to me. I was very surprised. I tidied my skirts as well as I could, covered my head, went to him, and bowed low. Such a fine-looking man. He must have been so handsome when he was young. Very tall. But his manner was rather austere… I was a little afraid.'

'Yes… Yes?' Naomi says. 'Go on.'

Ruth continues with her story. 'When he spoke his voice was stern and, I thought, curiously low. I must admit my knees were a bit wobbly; he had such a commanding presence. "I have heard about you," he said, gravely and I felt my heart beat faster, believing he had something against me. But then he said, "I hear you are the young woman from Moab who refused to leave our neighbour Naomi in the time of her loss. Instead of remaining in your own land with your own people, instead of returning to the house of your father, you chose to come here to be her daughter and to care for her?"'

'"Yes, sir," I told him. "I married her son and became her daughter. It is only right that I should fulfil my duty and stay with her. Besides, it is no difficulty to me because I love her as my own mother," I told him.'

And here Ruth smiles at Naomi who smiles back with watery eyes. 'And I love you, child,' she says.

'Well, I was afraid that the landowner would refuse to allow me to continue to glean since he knew that I was a foreigner. So I bowed low and asked that I might be allowed to continue to pick up what fell from the sheaves behind the reapers. And can you imagine what he said to me? He said, "I have heard that you are truly a daughter to Naomi. I have also heard that you do not have a man to watch over your affairs or to provide for you. I perceive that God is with you and so you are welcome in my fields." And then, mother, he smiled so kindly at me and invited me to spend all my time in his fields. In fact he advised me to stay close to his own women, and to drink from the same water jars. And he said that he had instructed his overseer to keep an eye on me so that I would not be molested by any of the men. I was overcome with gratitude. I could hardly believe such kindness, so I asked him how a woman from Moab could deserve such consideration but he did not answer. He just blessed me and wished me a rich reward. He spoke so beautifully, mother. He said that I had come under the wings of God for refuge. Isn't that a beautiful thought?'

Naomi, watching Ruth's face as she tells her story, sees the young woman's face more animated than it has been since before her husband died. Her eyes shine and her cheeks glow.

'You were very taken with him, weren't you, my child?'

Taken aback, Ruth looks at Naomi. 'But of course! He was so kind. I heard that he told his women to leave some stalks of barley especially for me. He even invited me to eat with him and he set aside a portion for me, this very food that I have brought home to share with you. I have not met such kindness before. Of course I am grateful.'

Naomi observes Ruth's flushed face. It has not occurred to her before today that while both of them are widows, Ruth's loss is very great. Naomi misses the physical comfort of having Elimelech close to her but she has more memories than Ruth, and she has known what it was to have children, even though she has lost them. For the first time she realizes that Ruth is still young enough to enjoy married life. If only it were possible for her to meet a fitting suitor. Naomi sighs. How impossible!

That night, having eaten better than she has done for days, Naomi sleeps more peacefully. But still she dreams. When she wakes she cannot remember her dream but she has remembered something else. Something important. Something that might redeem her shame and benefit her daughter-in-law. She is unusually animated the next day. Ruth watches her with concern. Naomi, trying to suppress her excitement says, 'My daughter, I have remembered why the name of Boaz sounded so familiar to me.'

Her wrinkled old cheeks are flushed, her eyes shine with a new light, the light of long forgotten hope. Ruth is surprised. She has not seen Naomi so spirited since those distant days when as very young girls she and Orpah were first brought to her mother-in-law's house to be married to Mahlon and Kilion. Happy days. Days full of hard work and laughter.

'He is a distant kinsman of my husband—distant but related nonetheless. Do you know what that means, my daughter?'

'No. I cannot think of what you mean, mother,' Ruth answers, puzzled.

'When Mahlon taught you the Law of Moses, did he not teach you the levirate law?'

'He taught me many things. He may have taught me this but I am ashamed to say I do not remember.'

'Then listen. According to this law it is the duty of the closest male relative to be the redeemer of the widow who has no other man to protect her. He is to redeem her lands and also to marry the widow in order to produce an heir and to continue the family name. I am too old now to have a son but you, my child, are still young enough. If Boaz is true to the levirate law you may be able to marry him and to bear a son and so redeem my shame.'

'Marry him? Marry Boaz? But mother, I am a foreigner here. And I am poor. Why should such a man even consider me?'

'He is a good man and a God-fearing man, you told me so. He is our kinsman. If he takes seriously the Law of Moses—if he does, and you have indicated to me that he may do so—then, dear Ruth, there is hope for us. Now, I have the beginning of a plan but I must give it more thought. When I've finally decided on a course of action you must do exactly as I tell you. For the present, do as he advised you. Be sure to work only in the fields of Boaz and to follow his women as they bind the sheaves. Even if you think another landowner's fields look better, stay in the fields of Boaz.'

Ruth is caught up in Naomi's excitement. 'He did look kindly on me. And he did tell me to remain with his women until they have finished the whole harvest, and he advised me not to go to any other field. He insisted on it, you know.' She clasps her hands together and shivers with delight at the new hope in Naomi's face, the possibility that they might be delivered from their desperate poverty, that they might be saved from the risk of disease and starvation which hangs over their heads. Not since her husband died has Ruth dared to hope for a better life. It is too good to be true. She cannot really believe that Boaz might consider marrying her, but now that she knows something of his obligation under levirate law, and because he has been kind even when he did not consider himself to be under any obligation, she hopes he may do something for them.

So Ruth returns to the fields of Boaz and works steadily every day from morning to evening. The store of grain in the shabby little hut grows higher day by day. Naomi and Ruth begin to look less emaciated. A gentle glow replaces their previous pallor. When the barley harvest is over the wheat is ready for gathering and Ruth works on. Naomi dries and winnows the grain and sets the best on one side to sell in the market-place. She is able to buy a new cooking pot, and seed to sow for crops. She even buys a goat, which makes Ruth clap her hands with delight. All the time Naomi considers the levirate law and Boaz. Boaz, kind as he is, does not yet know of his relationship to the two widows, of his obligation as kinsman redeemer to them. She has no doubt of his integrity, but how should she make him aware of his kinship? It will not do for a woman to sit at the gate with the elders to plead her cause. A woman who has no man to speak for her is in great difficulty. Since she has so recently returned from Moab she does not know a neighbour who could represent her at the city gate, who could take her petition and speak on her behalf.

By the time the harvest is complete, a plan has formed in Naomi's mind. It is a little bold, and her heart quakes at the audacity of her scheme. She will be putting Ruth in some danger, and if her idea does not work it will bring shame not only on her own head but also on Ruth's. The community might forgive Naomi, being old. But what of Ruth? Young, beautiful and foreign? Should she risk it? Naomi's courage almost fails, but then she recalls Ruth's words, 'Otherwise, what is to become of us?'

READY TO TRUST AND HOPE

On the last day of the wheat harvest, when Ruth comes home, Naomi calls her. 'This is what you must do,' she says. 'You must do exactly as I say.'

'Of course, mother. I will do anything you say. Why do you look so worried? The Lord God has blessed us so much in leading me to the fields of our kinsman Boaz. Think how much grain we have stored! Look at all the things that you have been able to buy in the market-place. Our situation is so much better than when we first arrived.'

'Yes, but now I am going to ask you to do something very difficult. More difficult than the work in the fields, gleaning from dawn to dusk. I know how hard that has been, but this is harder.'

Ruth is about to laugh. She cannot imagine anything harder than the way she has toiled over the past weeks in the hot sun. But she sees such concern in Naomi's eyes that she bites her lip. 'What is it? You know I will do anything you ask. I am your daughter now. Haven't I left my home and family, my country and my gods to come here to Bethlehem with you?'

'Then listen. Tonight Boaz will be winnowing his harvest at the threshing floor with his men. There will be much celebration and much wine.'

'Yes. I heard the women talking about it. Their men will not be home tonight. And tomorrow, when they do stagger home, they will have sore heads and red eyes. They will howl like wolves and sleep like lambs.' And here Ruth does laugh.

'My child, I want you to wash your hair and oil your body with the perfume we still have remaining in the little alabaster jar. Put on your finest robe and put on my wedding bangles and necklace. I have cleaned them for you—see how they sparkle. When you are ready I want you to go to the threshing floor.'

'The threshing floor? What do you mean? It is forbidden for any woman to go there.'

'Yes, it is. But I want you to go, dressed in all your finest clothes and perfumed and groomed like a woman of noble birth.'

'Mother! Dressed like that, and going to the threshing floor I would be worse than a prostitute! You cannot mean it!'

'Yes, child. I do. You must trust me. And you must do exactly as I tell you. Exactly, mind! I have thought about nothing else for days while you have been working in the fields. I am responsible for you. It is my duty to see you settled and to see that you have an opportunity to have a son.'

'Yes. But not like this! Surely, not like this?' Naomi is perturbed but not discouraged by Ruth's distress. She has thought and planned this strategy for too long to be put off now.

'Ruth,' Naomi says with an unusual note of authority in her voice. 'Listen carefully to me. Go to the threshing floor, but don't let anyone see you. Find a place where you can observe all that is happening. Then, when the men fall asleep, watch carefully to see where Boaz lies. When he is asleep, but not before, go and lie at his feet. Lift the blanket that covers him and lie down quietly. Don't wake him.'

'What should I do when he wakes?' Ruth asks doubtfully. Much as she loves and respects her mother-in-law she is scandalized at the plan. Naomi has always been most particular about matters of behaviour and morals. She is a woman of the highest integrity. Ruth simply cannot understand what has caused the older woman to come up with such an outrageous scheme. It is so out of character. Besides which, Ruth fears what might happen to her if she is caught at the threshing floor. Both she and Naomi would be dishonoured and ostracized. The men would have been drinking heavily; if they did see her, she was in danger of being raped. The possibility makes her shudder with fear. Also, she likes Boaz and she knows from his behaviour that he respects her. She does not want to do anything that might discredit her in his eyes.

'Don't worry about that. Just do as I say. Boaz will know what to do.'

'But, what shall I say to him?'

'You will know what to say when the time comes, child. Let us trust that the Lord God will be with you.'

BOAZ WAKES

Full of misgivings, Ruth obeys Naomi. It is dusk when, by the scant light of a crescent moon, and with her heart in her mouth, she makes her way to the threshing floor. Holding her breath she picks her way carefully up the steep pathway, guided by the glow of several campfires that circle the threshing floor. Groups of men sit guarding the grain and the oxen. Their voices, raised in animated conversation, raucous laughter and vulgar bursts of song, do nothing to calm her nerves.

'What am I thinking of? What am I doing here? Why has Naomi told me to do this foolish thing? Why didn't I argue with her? Whatever shall I say if I am seen?'

The last thought is so alarming that it all but persuades her to turn back. If she is seen she will be given little opportunity to speak or to say anything in her defence. As likely as not she will be stoned. With the full realization of this fact she stands still. She turns round. She will return, but what will she say to Naomi? Naomi, who loves her. Naomi, who said, 'Trust me'. Naomi, who said, 'Do exactly as I tell you. The Lord God will deliver us.' Ruth hesitates, turning first towards the threshing floor, then towards home.

She tries to remember all that Mahlon taught her about his God. 'Will he be with me, a foreigner? Will he deliver me? Is it his purpose to procure a protector-redeemer for us in this way?' She searches her heart for some comfort, some reassurance. There is nothing there, only fear. She seems to hear Naomi's voice, 'Trust me and hope for deliverance.'

With a slight shrug Ruth hugs her shawl more tightly around her shoulders and turns once more to face the glowing fires above her. Resolutely she continues on her way. Just in sight of the threshing floor she finds an outcrop of rock where she can hide and watch without being seen. At first she cannot make out what is happening. The men sit in groups around various fires, talking, eating, drinking and generally having a good time. Searching their shadowy forms she eventually spots the figure of Boaz. He really is a good-looking man, in spite of the hair greying at his temples. He seems to her to rise head and shoulders above the other men around him. Shivering a little she begins her vigil. She dozes a little at times, her head resting on the cold rock.

Gradually, the noise and activity around the fires subsides as one by one the men settle down, dark shapes against the glowing embers. Ruth, alert now, watches intently, straining her eyes until she catches a glimpse of Boaz retiring and, to her relief, to a quiet corner. When all the men are asleep she waits for a while, to be sure, then creeps between the sleeping forms, her eyes fixed on the spot where she saw Boaz settle, somewhat apart from the other men. Remembering the instructions given by her mother-in-law, she stealthily tiptoes up to him, lifts the corner of his sleeping-blanket and curls up at his feet. Tired out by the activities of the day, the tension and anxiety of carrying out Naomi's plan, she gradually falls asleep.

Ruth is awoken abruptly. In the middle of the night Boaz stirs, kicks out his feet, and finds a soft bundle curled up over them. Feeling with his foot he soon realizes it is a… woman! Taken aback he whispers hoarsely, 'What's this? Who are you?'

'Sir.' Ruth, shaken fully awake and bruised from his kick, trembles. 'Sir, it is me. I am your servant, Ruth. The daughter-in-law of your servant, Naomi,' she whispers.

'By the beard of my fathers, what are you doing here?' he hisses in the darkness.

'My mother, Naomi, tells me you are a distant kinsman, having the right of redemption over me by levirate law,' she answers quietly, shivering with fear.

In a low voice Boaz says, 'Is that so?'

The air is still. Sparks from smouldering embers, the movements of the restive oxen, the snoring of the men, all sound very loud in the silence. Ruth begins to think that Boaz has fallen asleep again. Indeed, she wonders if he was ever awake. Then, just when she thinks she will run away, she hears him draw in a long breath. Then to her amazement and relief he murmurs, 'God bless you, daughter, for your devotion to your mother and your loyalty to your husband's memory. You came to us a stranger, adopted our customs, and in everything behaved prudently. Everyone speaks well of you. A young widow like you might have behaved very differently. Now don't worry. I do have the right of kinsman redeemer but there is a closer relative than myself and I will enquire on your behalf to see if he chooses to exercise his right. If not, I will gladly do so.'

'Thank you, sir,' Ruth breathes with relief.

'Stay here for tonight and in the morning I will see what I can do for you.'

Ruth is too excited to sleep for a long time but the next thing she knows is that Boaz is shaking her gently.

'You must wake up,' he whispers. 'It would not do for anyone to see you here. Give me your shawl.'

Sleepily, Ruth obeys and Boaz pours six measures of barley into it, helps her to lift it to her shoulder, and sends her off home to Naomi.

THE BARGAIN IS STRUCK

While Ruth returns to the house of her mother-in-law, staggering under the weight of the barley, Boaz makes his way, deep in thought, to the town. He is more deeply stirred by the young Moabite woman than he cares to admit. Since he first noticed her on that day at the beginning of harvest, he has thought of her often. It is not simply her dark beauty. She also has a rare quality, difficult to define. Her devotion and loyalty to Naomi are remarked upon by all who know her but there is also that quiet determination, that refusal to be beaten down by her adverse circumstances that intrigues him. She reminds him of his own mother, Rahab. She has that same quiet singleness of purpose. The same perception. The same integrity and resolve. Boaz thinks now about his mother, and the ambivalent attitude of her neighbours when Boaz was a child. Rahab, the prostitute, on the one hand despised for her profession; on the other hand held in high regard because, trusting in the God of Isaac, she saved the lives of Joshua's soldiers when they went to spy out the city of Jericho. Because of her courage and faith Rahab and her entire family were spared when the city was overthrown. Boaz still has the red cord that was tied in his mother's window as a signal to the invading forces. Yes, Ruth reminds him of his mother. Rather to his surprise he finds himself reluctant to allow her closest kinsman to redeem her. As he walks on, deep in thought, a plan of action comes to mind.

Reaching the city gate where the elders and merchants transact their affairs, he is warmly greeted by everyone. Boaz is well respected both for his character and for his business acumen. Taking his place, he exchanges news with the elders concerning their harvests, their good and ill fortune. Eventually the man he is waiting for approaches the gate.

'Greetings, cousin,' he says, hailing him. 'Come and sit with me. I have some business to discuss with you.'

The man readily responds and joins Boaz, who continues, 'You are the closest kinsman of Naomi, the wife of Elimelech, who has returned to us from the plains of Moab. I have come to tell you that she has some land to sell. Since you are the closest relative the right of redemption belongs to you. If you wish to acquire it, tell me now before the elders of our people.'

'Certainly,' the man answers, always ready to increase his fields and livestock. 'I shall be glad to redeem it.'

'You understand,' Boaz says carefully, 'that in redeeming the land you acquire not only the property but also the widow of Mahlon, Elimelech's son? She is the stranger from Moab who returned with Naomi to live as one of us. It is your right and your duty to marry her in order to give her a son to perpetuate the dead man's name and his inheritance. She is a good woman.'

To his satisfaction Boaz observes the man's face cloud over. 'Ah!' he says studying his fingernails. 'Ah, yes.'

'She is, as I said, a fine woman. Hardworking...'

'I don't doubt it. No, I don't doubt it. A Moabitess, you say. Ah, yes. I should be glad to exercise my right of redemption. But it does, you understand, have complications.'

'I understand,' Boaz replies. 'Of course I understand. I need to know how you stand about this matter, however, because I am the next closest relative. If you are not willing, or not able, to redeem her, then the responsibility falls to me. This is why I have brought this matter to your attention before the elders. You have, as it were, a greater right than I do...'

'Yes. Yes. I appreciate your bringing it to my attention. But... it could be difficult. If I exercise my right of redemption, which, you understand, I should be glad to do... If, as I say, I exercise my right, it could create problems. I am the son of a wealthy man. We have not mixed our blood with strangers. You understand? I fear it could jeopardize my own inheritance if I were to take a Moabite woman to my home.'

'I understand.' Boaz answers quietly.

'But you, my friend. You are yourself the son of a foreign woman. For you it could make no difference. Since I hesitate to use my right of redemption, perhaps you would care to exercise the right yourself?' To Boaz' satisfaction, the man is almost pleading with him to release him from his obligation.

'My friend, if you have some difficulty in this matter, certainly I am ready to exercise the right. Are you sure this is your wish?'

'Yes, indeed. By all means. You can make good use of the land, no doubt.' And not waiting to hear the answer Boaz might give, he removes his sandal and hands it to Boaz in the presence of all the elders, thereby legally binding the transaction between the two men.

MORE THAN SEVEN SONS

The elders are well pleased with the affairs of the day. Some of them know more about Ruth than the kinsman of Boaz who has chosen to give her up. They know, as he does not, that she is not only beautiful but that she has qualities of character that more than match her beauty. Boaz is a popular man and the transaction delights them.

'We are witnesses to your contract, Boaz, and we give you our blessing as you fulfil the levirate law. We pray to the Lord our God that Ruth may be like Rachel and Leah, the mothers of the house of Israel. May she enrich your life, giving you many sons, and may she be like Tamar the widow, mother of our forefather, Perez. May your name live long in our land.'

The whole town joins in the celebrations. Ruth and Boaz, despite the difference in their ages and the difference in their experiences of life, clearly love each other. They have a mutual respect and regard for each other which touches the lives of everyone in their community and, not least, Naomi, who comes to live with them.

When eventually, from the joy of their union, Ruth gives birth to a son, Naomi takes the child into her arms, weeping tears of joy.

'A grandson! A grandson! I never believed I would see this day,' she exclaims.

The infant looks into her eyes. His face screws up into a puzzled squint and his mouth pouts open to reveal the tip of a tiny pink tongue. Naomi laughs with delight. The women of the neighbourhood come to see the child, declaring, 'There, you see, Naomi. Didn't we tell you everything would work out? The Lord God has not forgotten you. This child will comfort you in your old age. He will ensure that your husband and sons are not forgotten, and he will bring honour to your family. Praise God for the way he has blessed you and for your daughter-in-law Ruth. Look how much she loves you. Isn't she better than seven sons?'

Ruth and Boaz name their first son Obed, which means 'servant of God' and they trust his daily care to Naomi. She is no longer called Mara because from the time of Ruth's marriage her life is once again all sweetness and joy. The tragedy of her former years is forgotten. The home of Boaz is talked about as a place of such mutual love and affection that all who visit are welcomed. Friend or stranger, rich or poor, all are treated with equal regard. And every year, at the end of the harvest, the whole town—men and women, young and old—gather at the threshing floor to celebrate and to remember the goodness of God in the coming together of Ruth and Boaz. There is no king in Israel but in the days of Ruth and Boaz the land is at peace.

PRAYER

We thank you, Father in heaven,
for the ties of human love and affection.
Grant us the courage displayed by Ruth
when death separated her from the one she loved.
May we, like her, have loyal and open hearts
to enable us to grow and make new relationships.

If, like Orpah, we are not blessed with the strength
and spirit of adventure found in Ruth,
may we still know your blessing
in the quieter and safer paths of life.
Help us to grow in our understanding
of your goodness, tolerance and patience towards us
so that we, trusting in the redemptive power of Christ,
may accept others and ourselves as we are.
For Jesus' sake.
Amen

CHAPTER FIVE

IN SICKNESS AND IN HEALTH

His wife said to him, 'Are you still holding on to your integrity? Curse God and die!' He replied, 'You are talking like a foolish woman. Shall we accept good from God, and not trouble?'

JOB 2:9–10

See how the farmer waits for the land to yield its valuable crop and how patient he is for the autumn and spring rains. You too, be patient and stand firm... As an example of patience in the face of suffering, take the prophets... You have heard of Job's perseverance and have seen what the Lord finally brought about.

JAMES 5:7–8, 10–11

PROLOGUE

To all intents and purposes it was an ideal marriage. That's what most people thought. Wealthy and generous, Job and Jemimah had an endless stream of visitors arriving at their door. Kinsman or neighbour, foreigner or friend, all were greeted warmly. All were lavishly entertained. At the city gate, where the elders gathered to transact the business of the town, Job was known for his warm smile, his integrity and open heart. He never spoke ill of anyone. But neither was he afraid to speak out against any form of injustice. He treated rich and poor alike, without favour, so that many came to him to settle their civil disputes. Young men stood aside for him and the old men rose to greet him as an equal when he approached. Job was loved and respected by all.

And, as if this were not enough, he also went out of his way to help widows and orphans, beggars and strangers. Nothing was too much trouble for him. Indeed, Job had extraordinary compassion for his fellow man. Job feared God. Everyone agreed that Job was a good man.

There were those, of course, as there will be in any community who, having a bitter and jealous spirit, claimed that Job only absorbed himself in good works because it absolved him from spending too much time at home with his wife.

Jemimah was a good woman. No one could dispute that. She was not a beautiful woman but she was an excellent wife. Only...

It was a joyless marriage. Job had everything a man could wish for—good looks, good health, great wealth, a fine intellect, accomplished children, fertile land and many faithful servants. He even had the best gift of all, a thankful heart. But sadly he had a joyless marriage.

Job gave thanks for everything—even for his wife, Jemimah. She was a handsome woman who would have been beautiful were it not for her ungrateful, censorious spirit. She wanted for nothing but coveted everything. She envied her children their youth. She envied her servants their freedom from responsibility. She envied her husband his authority. She envied the moon for its silver light and the sun for its brilliance and warmth. In the winter she sat beside her warm fire and complained of the bitter cold. In summer she complained of the heat. She was indifferent to the perspiring servant who must stand behind her all day long, waving the enormous ostrich feather fan that Job purchased for her from Babylonian merchants. Jemimah had every blessing her heart could desire and wanted for nothing, but she did not have a thankful heart, so all her riches were worthless to her.

Any other man might have been troubled by such a partner, but Job thanked God for her. He thanked God that she was a strong woman who had borne and nurtured seven sons and three daughters for him; he thanked God for the way she managed the household; he thanked God, even, that her carping nature kept him humble, giving him cause to seek God's face for comfort. Job's wife was, beauty apart, everything a man might desire in a wife. She was hardworking and organized, conscientious and obedient, blameless and dedicated to the good works of her husband. Since she lacked great beauty, Job thanked God that other men did not lust after her. She managed the household efficiently and was respected, if not loved, in the community. In everything she was dutiful— but joyless. By little shrugs and sighs, like a running stream, she constantly murmured that life was a trial and a woman's work was never done. She gave such a subtle impression of being hard done by that those who spent time in her company had the sense that she suffered greatly, without knowing quite how or why.

JEMIMAH COMPLAINS TO HER SISTER

'It's not that I'm complaining,' Jemimah confides to her sister. 'I'm a fortunate woman. I know I am. I have a good husband. None better. It's just that... Well, everyone says that he is a good man. And, he is. It is just that sometimes he is too good. Too considerate and too caring. Of other people... I just wish he would spend a little more time at home with me. He seems to have time for everybody else. Everybody but me.'

'You are jealous!' her sister asserts, laughing.

'No! That's ridiculous. How could I be jealous? He is a good man. He serves the Lord God more faithfully than anyone else I know. And I also serve the Lord God, in my own way. I always welcome his visitors. I entertain them. I feed them. I make sure the house is clean and the clothes are mended. I spin the wool and weave the fabric. I fetch the water and cook the meals.'

'You have many servants and also slaves to do it, you mean!'

'And who has to oversee their work? I do. They can't be trusted to do anything without being driven. Besides, I have borne Job's children, fed them at my breast, helped them to take their first faltering steps, healed their hurts and watched over them in every way until they reached maturity.'

'And so you should!' her sister retorts. 'It's what we women do! And what fine children you have, Jemimah. Seven fine, healthy, good-looking sons and three beautiful daughters. You don't realize how fortunate you are!'

'Of course I do! Didn't I just say so? I have a fine family. The Lord God has blessed us in many ways through the years. But then, my husband Job has worked hard for his blessings. That's what I'm saying. I have a fine husband. Well respected in the town. Isn't he blameless? Doesn't everyone say so? And should not the Lord God bless him for it? Of course he should. My husband has worked hard for all his blessings.'

'And you are complaining about it?'

'No I'm not. I'm just asking, what about me? I do more than my fair share. Yes, the duties of the home are my responsibility, and I willingly accept them. I manage the household despite my lazy good-for-nothing slaves who have to be watched and beaten all the time. They wouldn't lift a finger if I were not behind them, endlessly goading them. I blame Job— they know he is altogether too lenient. No one knows what a hard time I have of it behind the scenes. He's altogether too good-natured and easy-going. Do you know, we have beggars from far and near calling at our house at all hours of the day and night? How would you like that? Not at all, I'll be bound. Job is known for his refusal to turn anyone away. So they tell their friends. I declare they do.'

'Then why don't you say something to him? Why complain to me?'

'I'm not complaining! When did you ever hear me complain? Besides, you just don't understand. Look, our sons and daughters are grown up now, you said so yourself. Grown men and grown women, able to take care of themselves, able to enjoy themselves. I could wish that Job might now find more time to relax and enjoy himself with me. Our children may be off our hands, but Job will not let go of them. Whenever they have a party, whenever they gather together at one of their houses to celebrate an anniversary, Job worries. He worries that after drinking so much they might blaspheme. He worries that they might fall into all manner of bad behaviour. It is foolish. My children would never do anything wrong. They know the right way to behave. We have taught them well. They are God-fearing, as you know, and if, when they are a little merry and become care-less in their speech, surely the Lord God will understand? Surely he won't hold it against them, seeing that their father is such a good man? But what do you think Job does?'

'I'm sure you are going to tell me.'

'Every time they have a party he hardly sleeps. He tosses and turns all night. At the crack of dawn, while it is still dark, in fact, he gets up just to offer sacrifices for his children. What do you think of that? I wouldn't mind so much but he disturbs me. And it's so cold at that hour. And the fire burns low.'

'He is a devout man, Jemimah. You are a fortunate woman to have such a husband.'

'Devout? I wonder, is he really devout? Do you think he would still be as devout if his situation were to be different? Supposing, heaven forbid, that he was as poor and wretched as the beggars that he feeds at our gates. Would he be so devout? Of course, I don't believe he offers sacrifices and worships the Lord God simply because of his vast wealth. But, sometimes I wonder, you know.'

'Oh, Jemimah, you exasperate me. You may be my sister but, really, you make me so angry sometimes. I can't sit here and listen to another word. You don't deserve your husband. Really you don't. And if I don't tell you, nobody else will.'

CATASTROPHE

In the distance Job sees the man, running, running. As he comes nearer, Job and his servants see the runner's distress. Fear, panic, and anguish in every feature. His face is twisted, his eyes protruding, his mouth gasping for air. Job recognizes him as one of his eldest son's servants, and runs ahead of his servants to meet him. Catching the now stumbling figure in his arms he gently lowers him to the ground.

'Fetch water,' he commands, as he bends over the stricken man. 'What is it? What has happened?'

When the man can speak his words come in snatches of gasping speech. 'My lord Job. The Sabeans came. My master, your son, was in his house, celebrating... with your sons, and your daughters... I was in the fields... with your servants... ploughing with the oxen—your donkeys were grazing nearby—when the Sabeans attacked. We fought them... but they killed your servants... they stole your oxen, and your donkeys, all 500 of them. And I am the only one to escape.'

While he is still speaking a cry goes up from one of the household servants, 'Job! Job! My lord Job! See, another comes running.'

Job, still holding the wounded servant, lifts his head to see yet another messenger running towards him crying out as he runs, 'My lord! My lord Job! The fire of God has fallen from heaven. I saw it. The sheep, and the shepherds, are burnt to ashes. I am the only one to escape. There was no warning. Everything was burnt up.' And the man falls on his knees, beats his chest and wails inconsolably.

Job, still holding the first servant, cannot take in what he is hearing. At that moment an old man on horseback gallops up, the horse snorting and soaked with perspiration, exhausted from a hard ride. With an effort the man dismounts, trembling, and bows low to the ground.

'Master,' he whispers, 'I have come with terrible news. I was with your servants, watching over the camels at the watering hole. Chaldeans came, three bands of them. We were outnumbered. We saw nothing, heard nothing, until they were upon us. Master,' the man shudders, 'I have to tell you. They have made off with the whole herd of 3,000 camels. I was sent to tell you, because I am old and I do not fight so well, Master.'

'What of my loyal servants?' Job asks quietly.

'Killed, my lord Job. All killed. I watched from the hilltop. There was nothing I could do, Sir.' And the old servant weeps.

'I understand,' Job answers and turning to his steward says, 'See to his horse. Give him food. And carry this man to the servants' quarters, and take care of him.'

Heavy-hearted, Job rises to his feet. By now the whole village has gathered and the people cluster around Job, murmuring condolences. Then they part like a field of corn in the wind as another servant, his face streaked with blood and mud, is seen approaching.

'What's this?' Job asks. 'Who are you? What news do you bring?'

Wide-eyed, the man cannot speak at first. He stares at Job while the crowd shifts uneasily.

'Tell me, my son. You have news for me? Some disaster to tell me? What can be more terrible than the misfortunes that have already befallen me on this evil day?'

'My lord.' The man tears his clothes in lament, throws handfuls of dust into the air and prostrates himself in front of Job. 'My lord, your sons and daughters were eating and drinking at your eldest son's house. A whirlwind blew up from the desert, moving like fire, destroying all in its path.'

A murmur of disbelief spreads through the crowd of onlookers.

'My children?' Job asks. 'What has happened to my children? Are they safe?' His voice is hoarse with anxiety.

'My lord, the whirlwind came with great power. It battered all four corners of the house. The house collapsed.'

'But what of my children? Never mind the house. What of my children?' The man is silent. He cannot meet Job's eye.

'Speak, man!'

'Dead. All dead.'

Now a loud cry goes up from the crowd. The women begin to wail and the men weep openly. Job tears his garment, throws himself on the ground and howls with anguish.

In the days that follow, Job shuts himself away and wrestles with his grief. Disbelief, anger, self-reproach—why didn't I offer more sacrifices? Guilt—why didn't I show my children a better example? Despair—why has God forsaken me? Job's feelings are in turmoil. Until, one day, he shaves his head, washes his body, dresses in clean clothes and then before all the people he prostrates himself in worship, saying, 'I came naked into this world, and naked I shall leave it. All that I have belongs to the Lord God. He gives and he takes away. In everything he is worthy of praise.'

JEMIMAH COMPLAINS TO JOB

But what of Jemimah? She has also lost everything she lived for. In the space of a day her life has been destroyed. She cannot believe she will not see her children come, laughing and chattering, over the hill towards her. She constantly raises her eyes to the horizon, searching for them. At times she is convinced she sees them there, shadows in the distance, making their way homewards. She is distraught. She can barely grasp the loss of all Job's wealth and their hitherto serenely comfortable life. She sees, as if in a dream, Job dismissing the servants, pleading on their behalf for rich neighbours and acquaintances to give them work. Everything is like a bad dream. Surely she will wake and find it is not true.

From the time that Job emerges from his grief, shaves his head and worships the Lord God, she finds him infuriating. How can he accept these disasters so calmly?

'"Blessed be the name of God"?' she screams at him. 'How can you bless his name? Hasn't he brought this trouble and disaster upon us? Why don't you curse him? Curse him and die!'

'That is how a fool of a woman would talk,' he says. 'If we take happiness from the hand of the Lord God, should we not also take sorrow?'

The days pass. Job steadfastly refuses to curse God. Neither does he deviate from offering prayers and sacrifices as he has always done. But his heart is heavy nonetheless, weighed down by grief. He is burdened by debt. He is stricken by his wife's anger, as he had hoped to find some comfort and strength as they shared their terrible misfortune together. As the days pass the shock of his sudden losses and the strain of his new situation wear him down. His health suffers. His feet and legs become swollen and infected. Gaping sores develop and cover them. Putrid abscesses appear in his mouth. His eyes become bloodshot. He cannot eat or digest even the simplest food. Painful boils spread over his whole body, disfiguring him. He looks to Jemimah for comfort.

'Don't come near me,' she spits at him. 'Your breath smells foul. Your body is disgusting. I can't bear to look at you. You are not the man I married. Why don't you curse God? Why don't you die and free me from my misery?'

'Your misery?' Job answers sadly. 'My dear, foolish woman, do you think I am happy to be in this state? Can't you find it in your heart to assist me just a little?'

'What can I do?' she bleats. 'I am only a feeble woman.'

'Find me some broken pots,' he answers. 'I will sit in the ashes of the fire and scrape the pus from my skin, to clean it. Perhaps then it will not be so offensive to you. And perhaps you would make sacrifices to the Lord God on my behalf, since I can barely walk to the altar myself?'

'I? Make sacrifices? He is your God. Why don't you curse him? Haven't you always worked hard to earn the blessings he saw fit to give you? So why has he deserted you now? What kind of god deserts a good man when he is in trouble?'

Job says nothing but turns his back on her and, shoulders drooping, walks away, painfully dragging his body to the ash heap. Here he sits, scouring his wounds with broken pots in an effort to clean them. He scrapes them until they bleed. He cannot sleep. He cannot wash. Jemimah watches him.

'What is happening to us? It must be a dream. Surely I will wake up and find it's all a bad dream,' she thinks. 'It can't be real.'

But it is real.

The Lord God has forsaken them. Why? What evil have they done? Why are they punished now? What sin could Job have committed to bring such disaster upon his house? Her husband is an upright man, Jemimah is sure of it.

Hardly aware of what she is doing, Jemimah prays, 'God of my husband Job, my sufferings are too terrible. I do not understand why you have turned against him, but do I have to suffer as well? I have done nothing wrong. You have taken away my children, the fruit of my womb, the light of my life. They were good children, simply enjoying a party together, not hurting anyone. Why did you send a storm from the desert to destroy them? I cannot bear it. Punish my husband, if you must, but why me? I do not know how he can bless your name when for no reason you hurl disaster on us and shower us with misfortune. I cannot bless your name; it would be dishonest. Why have you left me without comfort? Why have you forsaken me? I feel so alone.'

Then she screams at Job again where he sits, forlorn, in the ashes. 'Your god has found you out! Admit it, you have sinned against him. Ask forgiveness and perhaps he will restore us, then our neighbours will value us once more. You alone must say you are guilty, for I cannot help you and neither can anyone else.'

With these angry words she goes into her empty house and shuts the door. Darkness falls.

JEMIMAH SUMMONS THE FRIENDS OF JOB

They are glad to come, these friends of Job—Eliphaz of Teman, Bildad of Shuah and Zophar of Naamath. They are not able to admit it, but secretly they are rather pleased. How are the mighty fallen! Job, the devout man, has fallen from grace. It must be so. Why else would he be in so much trouble? The news travelled fast and they spent time talking with one another, speculating on what hitherto unknown flaw in his character has been his downfall. They can barely suppress their delight when they hear from Jemimah.

'Please come,' she said. 'I am at the end of my tether. I do not know what to do. I do not know what to say. Perhaps he may listen to you. Perhaps your words may comfort him.'

And so they come. Ignoring the beggar sitting in the ash heap, they hurry into the house.

'Where is he? Where is our friend?'

Jemimah looks at them. 'I can't bear to look on his sufferings so I busy myself about the household duties. What else can I do?' She goes to the door and points at the beggar.

'Look there!' she says bitterly. 'There is my husband. Don't you recognize him? What can I do to help him? I cannot bear to see him like this.'

Shocked, the three friends stand at the door and look at the bag of rags they have just passed. Vermin crawl over his body and feed off his scabs. His speech is wild and rambling, like that of a madman. Silently they regard their disfigured friend. Clearly the situation is even worse than they have heard.

'If I could only understand I would not complain,' Jemimah whines. 'I just do not know what has happened. He refuses to talk to me, so I called you. I reasoned that, since he will not speak to me, and since he will not listen to me when I implore him to repent, he might listen to you. You are his dearest friends.'

Eliphaz, Bildad and Zophar weep aloud and tear their robes. Throwing ashes on their heads in grief they sit in silence before Job for seven days and seven nights. In this way they think to share his sufferings. But it only makes Job worse. He is so depressed now that he will not eat. Finally he cries out,

'Oh God, I wish I'd never been born! What evil star shone on the night I was conceived? Why didn't I die in the womb, or at birth, or when my mother suckled me? Then I wouldn't have lived to see this day, I would have been spared all this agony, and this misery called life. It would be better to be dead. There is peace in death. Oh God, let me die!'

'Listen to him!' Jemimah wails. 'This is not the man I married. He is changed beyond all recognition. I have never seen him in despair like this. Oh, what shall I do? What is to become of me? Am I to wear a widow's garments while my husband is still alive? What kind of life is that?'

Now Eliphaz feels so uncomfortable that he cannot remain silent, he must find something to say. But what? And how? Gathering courage, he moves as close as he dares to Job, covering his nose against the stench, and asks cautiously, 'If I say something to you, will you bear with me? You are a man of faith, you know God is just. We are no more than moths in his presence, having no wisdom of our own. Who are we to question God? You must have faith!'

Since Job listens without comment his friend is encouraged to continue. 'Confess your sin and believe. Disaster only falls upon the arrogant. The proud are the authors of their own downfall. He who wounds will also soothe the sore, and the hand that hurts is also the hand that heals. Blessed are those whom God corrects! Six times he will deliver you from sorrow, and the seventh time, evil will not touch you. So, Job, you must be humble and patient before God.'

Jemimah is greatly impressed with these wise words, but Job does not seem to hear them. Then, with a sudden flash of anger he retorts, 'Who are you to speak on behalf of God? I have done nothing to deserve his punishment, but even so his arrows stick fast in me and my spirit absorbs their poison. You have no idea how much I suffer, nor why. If my words sound wild, is it so surprising? I would rather die than live like this. What is there to live for? God himself knows I have never rebelled against him. "Be patient," you say to me. I do not have the strength to be patient. You only want me to recover because you cannot bear to see my pain. Do you think you might be next? Why can't you leave me alone? Don't you think I am suffering enough without having your empty words, your vain advice, to deal with? I could cope with fair comment, but your words judge me. God alone is my judge.'

Now Bildad, feeling he must back up his friend, Eliphaz, joins in.

'Calm yourself, my friend. You are out of your mind with your suffering. We do understand. But consider this: can God be unjust? If your sons sinned against him, he has punished them for their wrongdoing. You for your part, if you are pure and honest, must now seek God, plead with him. Then his light will shine on you and he will restore you to health and your house to prosperity.'

Again, Jemimah wonders at the wise words. Surely Job will listen now? Bildad reminds Job to consider the lessons to be learnt from their ancestors, and to meditate upon the natural world.

'Consider these things,' he says. 'Look at the majesty and beauty all around us. God will not, cannot, reject anyone who has integrity. How can you think otherwise? It is your suffering which prevents you from understanding the truth. We are your friends. Listen to what we say.'

'Oh, he is such a wise man,' Jemimah thinks. 'He speaks such wonderful words. Surely now my husband will understand. Surely now he will fall on his knees and repent and surely, then, God will restore our fortunes. My children cannot be given back to me but the Lord God may give me more children. Who knows? If only Job my husband would repent.'

JOB'S ANGER

But Job is more rebellious than ever. 'How can I argue with God?' he demands. 'Can I stand before him in a court of law? What power could I use to bring my cause to his attention? Even if I am upright, what point is there in arguing with him? He would not listen to me. He crushes me without reason. He fills me with bitterness because I see that he destroys innocent and upright, guilty and wicked alike. What point is there in leading an upright life? It makes no difference to him. Besides, I am no longer sure myself that I am without sin. I no longer understand what it means to sin, or know the difference between good and evil. My soul is embittered. Yet in spite of everything I will plead my case before God. To whom else can I turn? Neither my wife nor my friends bring me any consolation.'

This unexpected outburst astounds Job's friends and for a moment or two they cannot think of anything to say. Then Zophar decides to try. But he has nothing new to say. He reminds Job again that the Lord God is wondrous great, mysterious and all-powerful. Zophar beseeches Job once more to reconsider and repent. He has, after all, admitted that he might be a sinner.

As he is speaking, a young man from the town comes to listen. When Zophar has finished this young man, Elihu, decides to have a go. 'I may be young compared to you,' he exclaims, 'and I had always believed that wisdom comes with age. But now I see that God can give wisdom to even a young man if his heart is open and his conscience clear. He wants me to tell you this: you are all wrong!'

And, with all the enthusiasm of well-intentioned but misguided youth, Elihu reiterates all that has been said already. The three friends are outraged, and even Jemimah feels somewhat insulted. And his words simply have the effect of adding to Job's anger so that he rages at all of them. 'How would you stand up to the suffering I endure if it happened to you? Do you think you are better than I am? Would your faith stand the test? Who are you to act as advocates on behalf of the Almighty? The Lord God does not need you to defend him. I will no longer listen to you. Instead I will remonstrate with God. He shall answer for himself. Let him kill me if he will, but I will speak. I was living at peace when he set me up as his target and shot his arrows at me from all sides. Now my life is worthless. If this is what my life must be, let me die. But first let me hear God give an explanation for my suffering.'

JOB'S WIFE PRAYS

Stunned by this outburst, Jemimah withdraws. She finds herself walking to the place where Job has been in the habit of offering sacrifices to Almighty God. When she gets there she prostrates herself on the ground. Words fail her. She does not know how long she remains like this. Then she finds herself praying, 'Oh, Lord of Hosts, creator of the world, how terrible it is to hear my husband's despair, to see him in such misery. How terrible to think he dares to challenge you, high and holy One. He has always been so strong, so confident, so assured. I am distressed because it was me who said, "Why don't you curse God and die?" I wish I had not said that. I spoke in haste because I was so upset. Lord God, the winds and the seas are in your hand. You see all things. You know all things. All power is yours. Deliver my husband from the desolation he is in. Deliver him from his torment. Be kind to him again, as you used to be, I beg you.

Remember, righteous One, he always considered the needs of others before his own. He never neglected the poor and needy. He sat at the city gate to listen to all who came with their troubles and disputes. Without fear or favour he gave his advice and counsel. Everyone who heard him respected his judgment. Even in all his troubles he has never turned his face against you. I have been guilty and I have forsaken your path, but Job my husband has never lost faith. I have been guilty of bitterness. I have found fault with those around me and I have been envious of others. I beseech you to have mercy upon me and not to consider my husband deserving of the punishment which rightly belongs to me. Why do you treat him as an enemy? Deliver him from his suffering and bring him again the joy of your salvation. Forgive me for my sin against him, I implore you, O Lord. Let him be well again and I will serve you faithfully and patiently, even as my husband does.'

EPILOGUE

Day after day, white-haired and wrinkled, old Job and Jemimah sit side by side at the door of their house. People come from far and near to sit with them, sometimes to talk, sometimes just to sit. They come to draw strength from this ancient couple who are renowned for their kindness and wisdom. All are welcome. But most welcome of all are the young children of the seven sons and three daughters borne by Jemimah in her midlife, when she thought her child-bearing days were past.

There is no more contented couple than Job and Jemimah in all the land. There is no man wealthier than Job, no woman more beautiful than Jemimah, no household more joyful. All the troubles and suffering they have endured have refined them as fire refines gold. Enduring much adversity together they have grown very close to each other. They have also matured in their knowledge and love of God. Jemimah, always handsome, now no longer bitter, has become radiant in old age. Her beauty arises from the inner wisdom of walking close to God. Her smiling face brings sunshine to everyone she meets and she is known for her ready laughter.

Those who have known them for many years marvel at the love they have for each other and at the generosity of spirit that marks their lives. In the villages it is said that no one stood by Job in the time of his adversity. No one believed him innocent. Even his closest friends sat in judgment upon him when he looked to them for comfort. But Job does not hold a grudge against them. Instead he burns sacrifices and intercedes on their behalf.

Job does not speak of the days of his suffering. 'It is behind me,' he says, 'and God is merciful.'

But sometimes Jemimah will confide in whispers to her closest friends, 'Job challenged Almighty God, you know, and in the mouth of a mighty storm he answered him. "Stand up like a man," God said, "and answer my questions. Do you have the power over the earth and all its creatures, as I have? Can you perform mighty deeds, as I can?" And my husband Job was humbled in the sight of the Lord God. Job says that before that day he only knew what others had told him, but now he has seen the truth of God with his own eyes. My husband has always been a righteous man but now he is also a humble man. No woman could wish for a more wonderful husband. I am the most fortunate woman alive.'

PRAYER

Almighty God,
Father of our Lord Jesus Christ,
Lover of all,
we bring to you the sufferings of the world.
We are silenced in the face of the terrible ordeals
that some have to endure.
We hold them up to your love.
Deliver us from trying to offer easy answers.
Give us grace, wisdom and courage not to turn aside
from the pains of those whose lives touch ours.
Teach us, in staying close to them,
to bring the pain it causes us to you,
And in so doing to understand more fully
the suffering of your Son, our Saviour, upon the cross.
Amen

LOSS AND RESTORATION

Israel, I will make you my wife; I will be true and faithful; I will show you constant love and mercy, and make you mine for ever.
HOSEA 2:19 (GNB)

Jesus heard them and answered, 'People who are well do not need a doctor, but only those who are sick. Go and find out what is meant by the scripture that says: "It is kindness that I want, not animal sacrifices." I have not come to call respectable people, but outcasts.'
MATTHEW 9:12–13 (GNB)

A GOOD MARRIAGE

When Gomer, daughter of Diblaim, married Hosea the prophet, there was great rejoicing. It was generally agreed to be an excellent match. Gomer, beautiful headstrong Gomer, a charming, lively, intelligent young woman and Hosea, passionate, handsome, industrious and scholarly. They were a fine couple, a credit to both their families and an asset to the community.

Hosea's devotion to Gomer was apparent to everyone. He watched her all the time, caressing her fondly with his eyes wherever she walked, whatever she was doing. Gomer, on the other hand, was more in love with the idea of love. Marriage to Hosea was, to her, a triumphant conquest. From a much admired and pretty child, she had matured into a fine-looking woman, accustomed to the adoration of all the young men in the village. All, that is, except serious, handsome Hosea. He was invariably aloof, apparently impervious to her stunning beauty. He always treated her courteously but with studied indifference. He intrigued her, challenged her, and she determined to find a way to enslave him. Her marriage was a conquest indeed. The old women nodded their heads sagely. Hosea would keep her passion in check, and light-hearted Gomer would limit his tendency to take life too seriously. Yes, it was a good match. The villagers rejoiced throughout the wedding week. True there were a few who shook their heads and warned of trouble to come. These perceived, perhaps, that Hosea's calm exterior masked a jealous and possessive disposition that would too severely suppress Gomer's carefree spirit.

One day, soon after the wedding, a terrible storm ravaged the village. Flashes of lightning lit the sky with an eerie blue light. Thunder crashed and echoed round the valley, shaking the buildings to their foundations, and whipping the trees so hard that it seemed they must be uprooted. Wild wind howled through the village, screaming between the houses and workshops and lifting the roofs off the cattle sheds. Children, waking suddenly from sleep, clung to their parents for comfort. And all night long the rain poured down upon the village until the dusty main street became a fast-flowing stream. The old men said afterwards that they could not remember such a storm in all their days.

At daybreak, when the storm had passed, the villagers came out to survey the damage in the warmth of the morning sun. It was discovered that one house had been struck by a bolt of lightning which had killed the inhabitants—Gomer's parents, her brothers and her sisters. All of them taken at one stroke. She was bereft, inconsolable.

It was often said afterwards that Gomer never really recovered from the shock of her sudden loss. She appeared to come to terms with her grief, but her face lost its rosy flush of happiness and her large eyes grew larger, like deep dark pools in her pale face—and her belly grew fat and round. She was with child. The neighbours sighed with relief. Life goes on and a child was just what she needed to take her mind off her loss. The Almighty God takes away and yet he still gives. It is in the nature of things.

Day by day as her belly grew larger Gomer's face grew paler. Eventually, just nine months after the wedding, Gomer gave birth to a fine baby boy with a lusty cry. God be praised! Surely the wagging tongues that predicted unhappiness must now be silent. Even in her loss Gomer was fruitful, and not only so, but her first-born child was a son. Hosea's name would live for ever. Once more there was great rejoicing in the village.

THE NAMING OF THE CHILD

But it was a surprise and a disgrace when Hosea named the child Jezreel. Why Jezreel? No one wanted to be reminded of the history of the city of Jezreel, where Ahaziah the King, Jezebel the Queen Mother, and every member of the royal family were butchered by Jehu, forefather of the present king. Why would Hosea choose to identify his own son with the constant reminder of this shameful event? It was shocking. An uneasy whispering drifted through the village. No one dared to voice their disapproval openly but behind closed doors, in the security of their own family circles, many asked the meaning of Hosea's choice. It was not long before Hosea himself answered the questions they dared not ask. He stood in the market-place and preached to all who would listen.

'Why are you shocked at what I have done? Don't you know that the Almighty God will avenge the murders committed by Jehu, the king's ancestor? It is the God of hosts who has given my son's name to me. It is a sign to you that before long the Almighty will punish the house of Jehu for the massacres at Jezreel, ending his dynasty and destroying Israel's power.'

When they heard this, the people were very angry. How dare he remind them of these atrocities? Terrible things done in the name of the Almighty God, and so long ago. It was history. How dare he say their king would be overthrown and their armies destroyed? And how could he burden his own son, his heir, with his gloomy predictions? It was disgraceful.

Seeing their resentment Hosea said to them, 'Don't you understand that I am a prophet of the Almighty God? This is the word which has come to me. It is up to you whether you listen or not.'

Then the people, offended by Hosea's words of prophecy, said that he must be mad. Who gave him the authority to say that he was a prophet? He was a man just like them, and they knew his parents. They turned their backs on him and refused to listen and so Hosea went off to preach to the villages and towns round about.

His neighbours noticed that it was from the time of Jezreel's birth that Hosea's behaviour began to change. Always serious, he now exhibited a huge zeal for God, preaching at every opportunity, everywhere. No matter where he was, Hosea would grasp opportunities to rebuke the people and warn them that the idols they made with silver and gold were worthless. 'Sow the wind and you will reap the whirlwind,' he admonished them. So it was that, though he made them very angry at times, his neighbours became aware that they did indeed have a prophet living among them. Sometimes they were rather proud of him, but at other times they were embarrassed. He made them uneasy because he constantly warned them of the trouble to come. They did not want to hear it; they were at peace and comfortable. Their lives were secure and prosperous. They had other gods for their protection, gods who did not make heavy demands upon them—unlike the Almighty God of their father Abraham.

Hosea's increasingly frequent absences were therefore something of a relief to them, but they looked with sympathetic concern on Gomer who was, they all agreed, becoming a shadow of her former self. For her part, Gomer was disconsolate. Marriage was not the joyful experience she had dreamed about. She was disillusioned and she had no one to whom she could turn for comfort. Hosea left her alone too often, and even when he was at home it seemed to her that he was distant. His fervour for the things of God consumed him, occupying all his attention and filling his every thought and word. He hardly seemed to notice Gomer and even when he made love to her she felt his mind was elsewhere. She felt worthless. When Hosea was away she began to take offerings secretly to the shrines of the Canaanite gods, beseeching them to make her more desirable to her husband.

The child Jezreel was barely a year old when Gomer gave birth again. This time a beautiful baby girl was added to the family. The neighbours wondered what she would be named but dared not ask. They did not have long to wait.

When the naming day arrived Hosea called the people together and stood in the market-place once more. In a loud voice he announced to his neighbours, 'See! Now I have been blessed with a daughter. But the word that comes to me from the Almighty is that she shall be called Lo-Ruhamah, "The Unloved", as a sign to you. God says, "I will no longer show my love to the house of Israel. I will not forgive them. I will love and save the house of Judah but not the house of Israel." This is the word that comes to me. Let all who hear it be warned.'

TENSIONS MOUNT

After this Hosea and Gomer became a source of conflict in the village and throughout the region where they lived. Some said that God was with Hosea but others ostracized him and his household. Gomer, accustomed to being admired and petted by everyone, found this new experience of rejection very hard to take. And it was not only for herself that she suffered. She ached with sadness for the shame her son and daughter bore because of the names Hosea had given them. She could not understand what was happening and gradually reached the conclusion that the God of Israel, who directed her husband's life, must be fierce and cruel. As a result, she turned more and more often to other gods, hoping to find comfort and understanding from them. And she also turned to the arms of any man who might be ready to offer her kindness and consolation. There were many who were only too glad to boast of their conquest of Hosea's wife—Hosea, the upright, outspoken prophet. Gomer did not understand these things. She was convinced, with each new suitor, that she had found her true love at last.

'My husband does not love me,' she would say as, during his frequent absences, she found solace in the embrace of her latest admirer.

'What a foolish man,' he would answer. 'If I were your husband I would not leave you alone as he does. You are too beautiful to be left on your own.' Her lover would whisper seductively as he kissed her on her ears, on her cheeks, on her mouth, 'Why don't you leave him and come away with me?'

'It's impossible. I am married and I have my two children to consider.'

'I will be a father to them.'

'No! No! I could not bear the disgrace. We would be outcasts.'

'We could go far away to another place where we are not known and make a new life together.'

So the arguments would go. Gomer longed to leave her husband and to escape her present life, but she knew instinctively that her lovers' words might not be trustworthy. At least with Hosea she had a home. She might not be happy but she was secure—and she knew it.

But Gomer was passionate. Poor, unhappy Gomer. She was also very naive. Every time she fell in love, which she did easily and frequently, she believed that, at last, it was 'real'. Here, finally, was a man who truly cared for her. Now she would find happiness. Young or not so young, Gomer found each of her lovers irresistible. In fact she found older men more appealing because, perhaps, she found in them the father she had lost and who had not been replaced in her husband.

It was inevitable that Hosea would find out. When he was away preaching, and while she was still nursing Lo-Ruhamah, Gomer was dismayed to discover that she was pregnant again. The child in her womb was not Hosea's. She knew it and it was inevitable that Hosea would also know it. He had been away too long and it would be impossible to hide the truth. Gomer realized, with a kind of dreadful relief, that she could no longer deceive him. The lover who fathered the child had long since left her. In fact Gomer was not at all sure she could say which of her lovers was the father of the child. There had been so many. Too many. And although she trembled to know she must face Hosea with the truth, she did not doubt for a moment that he would accept the child. What else could he do? He would be angry, of course, but perhaps he would understand, at last, how lonely and neglected she felt. Hosea would not shame her in public, she was certain of it. How could he shame her without also bringing disgrace on himself? He would not—he could not—he was a proud man. True, some of their neighbours might wonder and whisper. Let them. With that strangely contrary confidence of many an adulterer, Gomer was confident that her husband would forgive her. She was wrong.

Hosea's anger came as swiftly and violently as a summer storm but, unlike a summer storm, it did not pass. Never for a moment had he considered that his wife might be unfaithful to him.

'With child?' He could not take it in. He was stunned. He was like a man overcome by sudden blindness. He just could not believe it. And, like a blind man, he found his once familiar world strange and alien. Nothing made sense to him. Gomer watching him, realized, too late, that she had struck him a mortal blow. But she could not undo it. She could not change anything. Her confidence that Hosea would forgive her was shattered. How could she have been so foolish? As the child stirred in her womb Gomer finally became aware of her vulnerability. She longed for the child to go away.

Hosea was crushed. Angry, disbelieving, and hurt as he was, he could not understand what had gone wrong. Gomer had betrayed him, but he still loved her, adored her. How was it possible? For all her high spirits and flirtatious ways, his trust in her had always been absolute. Never for a moment, in his necessary and frequent absences, would he have believed her capable of being unfaithful. Surely she understood it was his duty to be away from home, preaching and warning the people to return to the Almighty God? Of course, it was not an easy calling, but it was what he had to do. It was the task given to him. Surely Gomer understood the sacrifice he had to make in his obedience to the call of God? Just as he had made sacrifices to obey his calling so she had been obliged to make a sacrifice too. It had been her duty to wait patiently at home, caring for the children, attending to the household and tending her vineyard. If it was lonely for her then surely she understood that it was also lonely for him? He had not expected more of her than he had expected of himself. How could she have betrayed him? For the first time he looked at Jezreel and Lo-Ruhamah with questioning eyes. Were they his children? He was no longer sure. Hosea was heartbroken. And besides all this, she had made him a laughing stock before his neighbours.

'How could I have been so stupid?' he asked himself. Why had Gomer betrayed him? Why had God allowed it? Why had such shame come to the house of his servant? Was not Hosea the mouth of the Most High, calling the people to repent and return to the God of their fathers, the God of Moses?

Hosea felt that not only had his wife betrayed him but his God had also betrayed him.

Hosea prostrated himself before God. He wept and covered his head with ashes. He tore his garments. And in his despair Hosea began to understand how the people of Israel had forsaken the Almighty God in the same way that Gomer had forsaken him. He began to understand at last something of the love which God felt, something of the pain, something of the longing which the Almighty had for his people. Hosea was overwhelmed with a truth too difficult to grasp in its entirety. Intuitively he perceived the spirit of God hovering over and around him and his tumultuous emotions were momentarily stilled.

GOMER LEAVES HER HOME

It was to be expected that Hosea should banish Gomer from his house. But in compassion for her he allowed her to delay until the child was born. Segregated from the rest of the household for the last months of her pregnancy, she remained until she gave birth to a baby boy. Another son. But this time the neighbours did not rejoice. It was well known that the child was not Hosea's son. And so, like Hosea himself, the neighbours began to wonder if Jezreel was really Hosea's true heir. There were those who smiled behind their hands. 'How are the mighty fallen!' But others were deeply troubled to see such disgrace visited upon a family who were previously held in high esteem. A young couple who had set out with such promise, with such high hopes. It was too bad, too sad.

No one offered to stand by Gomer. Hosea, too, was quietly ostracized. If anyone felt able to judge the rights and wrongs of the situation, no one was prepared to risk expressing an opinion. With barely suppressed apprehension the village waited to see what would happen.

They did not have long to wait. Although the new baby was not Hosea's natural son, he was prepared to accept some responsibility for the infant. He would not abandon the three children in spite of their mother's wickedness. Hosea named the new baby Lo-Ammi, 'Not My People', and he engaged a village woman of blameless character to care for the children. Gomer he sent away, alone.

'Where am I to go?' Gomer wept. 'What is to become of me?' She was on her knees, pleading with him.

'You should have thought of that before you shamed me,' he replied harshly. She did not look up and see the agony on his face.

'My husband, do not do this to me. I will change, I promise you. I will never look on another man again. Do not send me away,' she begged him. 'Where am I to go? What will become of me?'

'What will become of you? What has already become of you? That's what you should be asking. You have prostituted yourself and you are no longer my wife. Go to your lovers. Let them take care of you.'

In a last desperate attempt to save face she snapped angrily, 'They will. Yes, they will. They will give me food and water. They will give me wool and linen. They will give me all the olive oil and wine that I need. I will go to them!'

'Then go!' Hosea was torn between grief and anger.

'Give me my children and I will go,' she demanded, defiantly.

'The children stay.'

'No! No!' She had not foreseen that Hosea would want to keep her children. 'You cannot take my children from me!'

'I am not taking them,' Hosea answered with icy finality. 'You are leaving them. There is no place for you in my house. You have shamed me. You are no longer my wife and I am no longer your husband. Your children will be well cared for, but they will know themselves the children of a shameless woman. Your disgrace is upon their heads. Go!'

Hosea turned his back on Gomer and walked away.

As she watched him go Gomer realized at last that Hosea had grown immune to her charms. The full cost of her promiscuity began to dawn on her, but whatever remorse she felt soon gave way to fear, and fear to anger. It was not long before she had persuaded herself that she had been wronged and so she allowed herself to feel outraged. How dare he turn her out of her home? How dare he keep her children? She was still his wife. Hosea was to blame for everything that had happened. He had left her alone. He had no feeling for her when her family was killed in the storm. When her first child was born she had no mother, no sister, no one to turn to. They were all taken. She was left alone with her baby, feeling as helpless and bewildered as her infant. Hosea had not understood. Although she had received help from her neighbours, she felt it had been given grudgingly. She believed they had been reluctant to become too involved with the wife of the prophet. And, she reasoned, it was because Hosea called the child Jezreel. It was after that she had noticed people avoiding her. They made excuses and crossed the market square or disappeared into their houses whenever she approached. Hosea was responsible. Hosea and his God.

By the time Gomer left her home and made her way, barefoot, to the temple of Baal, empty-handed, and wearing only a simple tunic, she was convinced that she had been wronged. Hosea had sent her away all but naked, without a cloak and without any jewellery. Yet it did not matter, she told herself. She was still beautiful and that was all that was required. Prostitution was a lucrative profession in the temple and the priests took good care of the women who served the god Baal, at least for as long as they retained their seductive allure. When this failed it was only the fortunate ones, the wise and wily women, who were retained to initiate fresh young girls into the temple rituals. Gomer was confident that she would do well. She had to prove to Hosea that she did not need him.

But the temple prostitutes were better prepared and more skilled than Gomer in their trade and it was not as easy as Gomer expected. She could not admit it but she was not happy in her new situation. She missed her children and the comforts of her home. And Gomer certainly could not admit how much she really missed Hosea. She would never admit that. Never!

HOSEA'S GRIEF

Hosea nursed his sorrow in private. In public he continued to preach. Not only did he preach but he also confounded his neighbours by openly proclaiming Gomer's disgrace. Had he no shame? Had he no feelings?

They watched him. They listened to him. By careful observation they perceived that he did indeed have feelings. He was grief-stricken. But he used his shame and heartache to explain to the people the truths concerning God.

'See how my wife has deceived me,' he said, 'although I loved her. You are witnesses to my love. You were here when we were married and you joined in our celebrations. You have all seen my devotion to her. I loved her and planted a vineyard for her. No husband could have done more.'

Hosea's eyes filled with tears as he spoke. The people were moved with pity, but Hosea did not want their pity.

'And how has she repaid me?' he shouted passionately. 'She has deceived me. She has mocked me. She has played the harlot. Her children are not my children and they carry her disgrace with them.'

Hosea tore his robe before all the people and beat his chest. 'I have been wronged. What am I to do?'

The people shuffled uncomfortably. The man was demented. Serious, reliable, scholarly Hosea was behaving like a raving lunatic. And who could blame him? It was true. Gomer had behaved shamefully. They murmured amongst themselves, 'It was to be expected. He was away too often.'

'No, she wronged her husband, there can be no excuse.'

'She was always wanton. Even as a child.'

'She was too beautiful. That's the tragedy of it.'

So the people muttered together, some taking this view and some taking the other. None of them was prepared for the prophet's next outburst.

'You! You! You, the people of Israel, all of you, are just as guilty! You are no better than my whoring wife!'

A stunned silence greeted his remarks. What was he saying? What could he mean?

'I tell you, you are like my unfaithful wife,' Hosea continued. 'God's word came to me saying that you, his people, are like an unfaithful wife. You lie and cheat, you get drunk, break your promises, fight and steal, commit adultery and murder. You do not remember the God of Moses who delivered you from the hand of the Pharaoh. Even your priests lead you astray. Because of this the land will be cursed. It will dry up and become barren.'

If the people had not feared Hosea as a prophet, they would have stoned him there and then.

For many months Hosea went about warning the people of the danger they were in and pleading with them to return to the true God. Everywhere he travelled with his terrible message the people rebelled against him, hating him and calling him mad. He had few listeners and no friends. As he travelled from place to place he had a great deal of time to think about Gomer, remembering the happy days when they were betrothed, before they were married. How proud he had been that Gomer had chosen him! Of all the young men who desired her, she had chosen him. He had hardly been able to believe it. But was she deceiving him all the time? Did she marry him only because he could provide her with security, with a respected position in the community? Was she cuckolding him all the time, making him a laughing stock? He turned it over and over in his mind, finding it hard to believe that was so, but finding it equally hard to face the explicit evidence of her adultery every time he looked at Lo-Ammi. The boy had large dark eyes framed by long black curling lashes, just like his mother's, and he would fix the prophet with such a mournful gaze that Hosea found himself speaking unkindly to the child, as if he were responsible for his mother's disgrace.

Hosea's health declined as the months passed. By various means news of Gomer's unhappy life in the temple filtered through to him, increasing his despondency. She was a slave, he heard, by turns beaten, starved and abused. She was at the mercy of corrupt priests, and the lewd behaviour of perverted men—and women. It was too terrible. He tried not to think about her. He tried to convince himself that it was her own fault. He struggled to be pleased that she was being punished for her behaviour. But he could not. All the time he burned with desire for her. Waking and sleeping he ached for her. He longed for her.

THE COST OF FORGIVENESS

As the days dragged by, Hosea's struggle continued. His prophetic fervour increased, his yearning for his wife persisted, and he became haggard and emaciated. And then, imperceptibly, a strange transformation began to take place. His insight deepened and he saw more clearly that, just as he longed for Gomer, so God longed for his people. Just as Gomer had cheated on her husband, not understanding how much he loved her, so Israel had cheated on the Almighty God. And slowly Hosea perceived that God never stopped loving and longing for his people to return to him. Why else had Hosea and the other prophets been sent to preach repentance? Hosea began to understand that if the people would turn back, burn their idols and worship the Almighty God with pure hearts once more, they could yet be restored. The love of God was so great that if only his people would return to him they could be healed and could bloom like flowers in the desert. As Hosea began to understand this, so a glimmer of hope stirred in him. However bad things may be, they could change. As he mulled over these truths he finally conceived a daring plan.

When Hosea the prophet went to the temple to buy back his wife Gomer, daughter of Diblaim, there was a great commotion in the village. It was truly a remarkable occasion. Such a thing had never been done before. Hosea proclaimed his intention in a loud voice throughout the region for many days. The news caused such a stir that it spread rapidly. Everyone knew it. Everyone except Gomer.

Gomer was wretched. There was no denying it. The appalling life she was forced to live in the temple totally broke her rebellious spirit so that she was now convinced that she had been much better off as Hosea's wife. For although she thought herself lonely then, in the temple she came to know the desolation of true loneliness. She was desperately lonely, though never alone. She was always in the company of the women of the temple, or called upon by the priests, or allocated to gratify the desires of those who visited the temple. She mourned for her children. She was without hope.

When she heard a great commotion in the temple court, she took no notice. Neither did she rouse herself when women came, calling her name.

'Gomer! Gomer!'

She did not answer. Let them call. She no longer cared. She did not want to see them.

'Gomer! Gomer!'

She would not answer. Let them beat her. It no longer mattered.

Outside the temple the people were running here and there, pushing and shoving to get a better view.

'Come and see!' they cried. 'Come and see! The prophet has come to buy back his wife.'

'To buy her back? What for? What use is she to him now?'

'Does he plan to beat her? In public? Does he have another message for us?'

Some laughed. Some were shocked. Some were uneasy. All were curious.

'How much is he paying?'

'Not a lot, I'll be bound. She's soiled goods.' Raucous laughter greeted this remark.

No one knew how much Hosea was prepared to pay for his wife or what he meant to do with her. No one knew whether or not the priests would sell. For, when all was said and done, Gomer was still a valuable woman. She was still pleasant to look at and, though she may have lost some of the bloom of youth and her lively spirit may be more restrained, she was still an unusually interesting woman. Besides, the priests of Baal were shrewd businessmen. The very fact that it was her husband who came to buy her back would raise her price.

Never had such a thing been known. The whole town was agog. The crowd pressed forward, up the steps of the temple and into the courtyard. They heard nothing of what passed between the priests and the prophet until a whisper began to spread like wind rustling through the trees.

'Hosea has bought back his wife for fifteen shekels of silver.'

'...and also a measure of barley.'

'...and also a skin of wine.'

'The price of a slave!'

'Yes, Hosea the prophet has paid the price of a slave to buy back his wife!'

This was news indeed.

Proud, noble Hosea, and vain, conceited Gomer were publicly disgraced, shamed in the eyes of all who knew them. But once more, opinion was divided.

'It is a sign of greatness in Hosea that he has not been afraid to do this thing.'

'No doubt he has his reasons.'

'No, he loves her. He is a good man.'

'Perhaps. But we all know Hosea. He is a prophet.'

'You may be sure he has a good reason for his behaviour. He always does.'

'That's true. No doubt he will be telling us that this is an example of how much the Almighty God loves his people.'

'Perhaps he will... and perhaps it's true.'

At this the people were silent and one by one they began to drift away.

THE REDEMPTIVE POWER OF LOVE

And what of Gomer? What did she make of it all? She chose to ignore the commotion going on outside the women's quarters of the temple until one of the priests summoned her. She was expecting to be given to a man—a traveller, a Baal-worshipper, or a priest. It made no difference. She must obey.

Heavy-hearted and keeping her head lowered, she made her way to the antechamber where the priest would be waiting to instruct her. She did not care to see the man, so she stood, waiting for him to speak or to touch her. The man was motionless, and silent. Even now she did not raise her eyes. The silence was long.

'Gomer.'

That voice! She caught her breath, swayed, felt weak. He had called her by name. She recognized the voice but believed it was a delusion. Yet her heart beat faster, her legs grew feeble and beads of perspiration broke out on her forehead. The voice was so like the voice of Hosea, but it could not be. Then she heard it again.

'Gomer, I have come to take you home.'

Gomer could not breathe. Slowly she lifted her head and found herself looking into the face of her husband. Then her knees did give way and with a little cry she fell to the floor. Hosea made as if to move, but thought better of it and remained impassively where he stood. Gomer recovered, but remained crouched on the floor at his feet, shivering.

'My husband?' She could hardly speak.

'Yes, Gomer. Your husband. I have come to take you home.'

'But… but… how can you? I belong here. I have… I have… given myself to the temple… to the priests. You must know what I am.' Her breathing was laboured. Hosea's feet grew wet with her tears. 'Even if I could leave,' she wept, 'you could not take me back now. I am defiled.'

'You are free to come with me. I have paid the price the priests were asking for you.'

His voice was cold but it stirred turbulent emotions in Gomer. She struggled with disbelief, shame, relief, and hope—just the faintest glimmer of hope. Would he—could he—take her home? Was she dreaming?

'You cannot want to take me back after all I have done—what I have become.' Her voice was barely audible. 'You cannot mean it? I have been so bad… so very bad… so foolish.' Her voice faded.

'Gomer.' Hosea's voice was no longer cold but as tender as when they first married. 'I love you. I know you've wronged me. I was hurt, angry and shamed. I thought I could never forgive you. But I love you, Gomer. I want us to start again. Whatever you have been, whatever you are, you are still my wife. You are still the only woman I love. I want you to come home.'

Gomer began to sob without restraint. 'How can you love me, after all I've done?'

'I do love you.'

'And you will take me home?'

'Yes.'

'And the priests will let me go?'

'Yes.'

'You have paid for me?'

'Yes.'

Hosea stooped down, took her by the elbows, and lifted her to her feet. She could hardly see him through her swollen, bloodshot eyes. After a moment's hesitation he put his arms around her. She was tense and unyielding in his embrace but he held her close.

'Hosea.' She whispered his name with difficulty. 'I am sorry. I feel so ashamed.'

'It is not going to be easy, Gomer. But I am prepared to forgive you.'

'I don't deserve it. I am wicked. But I will try. I will try… to be better. Will you… help me? I want to be a better wife.'

'And I will try to be a better husband. I will not leave you alone so often.'

'You…' she hesitated. 'You have given up… preaching?'

Hosea almost laughed. 'No. I cannot give up proclaiming the word of God. It is what I have to do. But in future you will come with me on my travels. You will be part of my work. Our love will be a testimony and a witness to the people. A message they can see and understand of how much God loves his wayward people.'

'But what of Baal? I have been a servant of Baal.'

'And has Baal taught you what it means to be loved?'

'No,' she said. Then more decisively, 'No. he hasn't.'

When Hosea the prophet left the temple of Baal with Gomer his wife by his side, the people were astonished. Hosea said to them, 'You are amazed at what I have done because you do not really understand love. I am taking my wife back to our home because I love her with all my heart. She is sorry for the way she has been living and I have forgiven her. She will live with me, care for her children, grow wheat and vines. Gomer will bloom like a lily once more. Listen to what I say and understand what you see me doing now. I am walking hand in hand with Gomer, my wife. And you, the people of Israel, must learn to do the same. Turn away from false gods and false teaching and return to Almighty God, who loves you and longs for you, just as I love and have longed for Gomer.'

And so it was that when the people saw how much Hosea loved Gomer the daughter of Diblaim and considered all the things that the prophet said, some of them turned their backs and walked away but others, moved by his example of love, returned with joy to the faith of their fathers.

PRAYER

Holy God, our Father in heaven.
Your Son taught us that we should love our neighbours as ourselves.
We love imperfectly.
We barely know how to love ourselves
So we cannot know how to love our neighbours.
As husbands or wives, as parents or children,
As friends or strangers, as citizens or neighbours,
Teach us to love.
As we read and consider the love of Hosea for his wife Gomer,
Being a pattern of your love for Israel,
We remember you gave your Son, Jesus, as
A pattern of perfect love.
Fill us with love.
Amen

CHAPTER SEVEN

THE REFUGEE FAMILY

Joseph son of David, do not be afraid to take Mary home as your wife, because what is conceived in her is from the Holy Spirit. She will give birth to a son, and you are to give him the name Jesus, because he will save his people from their sins.
MATTHEW 1:20–21

I saw the Holy City, the new Jerusalem, coming down out of heaven from God, prepared as a bride beautifully dressed for her husband. And I heard a loud voice from the throne saying, 'Now the dwelling of God is with men, and he will live with them.'
REVELATION 21:2–3

THE TONGUE IS A FIRE

There's something wrong in the village. Not something obvious but an intangible foreboding. A cloud hangs over the normally tranquil community. Restrained whispering fills the corners of fields and workshops, the places where people gather to go about their daily chores. Something is wrong but nobody knows what and nobody knows who to ask. On the surface life continues, the busy but unhurried everyday routine. Smells of village life impregnate the air; from goat droppings, from animal skins hanging out to dry, from the sweet fermenting grapes, from aromatic spices, hot peppers, baking bread and braising meat. The women collect water, hang out bedding, sweep the floor, prepare the food, meet at the washing place and perform the hundred and one tasks required to keep family life running smoothly. They chatter and gossip in the ordinary way of women. The men, too, go about their business, ploughing the fields, herding the livestock and meeting to discuss communal affairs at the end of an industrious day. Joseph no longer joins them. He has been missing for days, shut away in his workshop, intent on some vital task. No one asks him why he is absent or what absorbs him so much. In this feverish atmosphere, gossip thrives.

Mary, the daughter of Joachim and Anna, has changed, they say. No longer the simple, happy child they all knew and loved, she has grown pale, become withdrawn. She is rarely seen outside her home and goes early or late to the well, shunning the company of the other young women. True, the girl carries out her duties as carefully as ever but without her normal gaiety, her lightness of spirit. Her mother also avoids contact with her neighbours, and says nothing. Despite her reticence the neighbours cannot refrain from expressing an opinion whenever they meet.

'The child is excited about the wedding.'

'She is nervous, as any young girl would be.'

'Yes, it's natural. I remember how I felt in the weeks when I was betrothed, after my marriage price had been agreed, and before the wedding week.'

'Oh yes, and so do I!'

There is general laughter and chattering as each woman recalls incidents concerning her own marriage. Then there is a lull in the conversation and someone says, 'My husband said he saw Joseph weeping!'

'What?'

'Are you sure?'

'How is it possible?'

The woman who made the confession looks uncomfortable, blushes, and begins fiddling with the edge of her shawl. 'I shouldn't have spoken.'

'What do you mean? Tell us.'

She refuses to answer.

'Tell us, wife of Juda, tell us. What do you mean? Why shouldn't you speak?'

'If it's true...'

'I cannot tell you. I promised my husband I would say nothing.'

Despite much cajoling, the wife of Juda remains silent and when Anna, the mother of Mary is seen approaching, she hastily retreats from the group to take refuge in her house. The wave of eager speculation is hushed as Anna draws nearer to the group, walking head down, as if to pass by. A watchful silence is broken when someone calls out,

'Hello, Anna. We've missed you. You must be busy about the wedding preparations?'

Hardly lifting her head, Anna replies, 'Yes, there is much to do.'

'And Mary, how is she? She must be very excited, with her betrothal agreed?'

'Yes, of course.'

'All is well?'

'Of course.'

'Stay and talk with us, Anna.'

'I cannot. There is much to do.'

The brief answer silences them.

Anna walks rapidly on, her troubled face giving the lie to her words. Close as she is to her neighbours, she is not yet ready to share her fears. The truth is, she is very worried. Mary has changed. She was always a serious and thoughtful child, and yet serenely happy, chattering away to her mother about anything and everything. But recently she has grown secretive, moody and, allowing for the natural apprehension she must be feeling, she seems excessively nervous. Anna is at a loss to understand it. Mary assures her mother that there is nothing wrong. Anna tries to discuss it with Joachim but he just laughs, saying that women are all the same, not happy unless they can find something to worry about.

LOVE ALWAYS TRUSTS

Mary's betrothed is Joseph. Joseph, the stranger, the southerner. Joseph, the carpenter from Jerusalem who arrived in this northern town with his widowed mother and sisters, not many years since. He is a man the villagers have come to respect for his honest labour and devotion to the Law of Moses. If asked, he says he left Jerusalem because he could not bear to work for the Roman soldiers and, if pressed further, he says he could not continue making the terrible wooden crosses upon which his countrymen were executed. To refuse to do the work was to invite imprisonment—or worse. Although the hills of Galilee are known to be the hiding place of Zealots—patriotic Jews intent on overthrowing the Romans by violent means—Joseph feels more at ease with himself in this remote region. He is a peace-loving man and here he can use his skill for purely constructive ends. He makes door lintels, ploughshares, gates for the sheepfolds and, best of all, he likes to wander in the surrounding countryside choosing the best trees and saplings to fell for his work. On their arrival here Joseph's family soon became close friends of Joachim and Anna, who were also immigrants from the south. It was the most natural thing in the world that Joseph should become engaged to Mary, their eldest daughter.

While the village speculates, Joseph hides away in his workshop. Sometimes a tear rolls down his cheek. He blinks impatiently, and brushes it away with the back of his hand. In his distress he cuts through thick planks of wood so effortlessly that he might be breaking bread. This normally mild-mannered man viciously kicks aside the off-cuts of wood, stamping angrily on the sawdust. Tortured emotions cloud his face. He goes over and over his last meeting with Mary, reliving each painful moment. Every detail of the day is etched on his heart, a day which has changed his life for ever—or so he believes. He sees it again now...

It is mid-morning. Joseph is busy planing a length of wood when Mary bursts into his workshop. This is extraordinary. No woman, not even his mother or sisters, dares to venture into this, his private place. Indeed, few men would presume to do so without an invitation or without having a particular request to make of him. Apart from being his place of business, it is also his retreat from the world. Here, as he cuts and crafts wood with tender care, he chants the psalms of David under his breath and thinks deeply about the world in which he lives, the history of his people, and the Roman governors who presently rule the land promised to his fore-fathers. He longs for Messiah to come and deliver his people.

And yet here is Mary, his betrothed, bursting into his haven without warning and without shame. She is in an alarming state. Her eyes sparkle unnaturally, her cheeks are scarlet, her hair is windblown and her clothes dishevelled. She leans against the doorpost, panting for breath.

For a moment he just stares at her, unable to believe what he sees. Quickly recovering he puts aside his tools and strides over to her. Gently but firmly placing his hands on her shoulders he asks, 'Why Mary, what are you doing here? What's wrong?'

He fetches a stool and helps her to sit down. Gratefully she sinks on to it and, leaning forward, gasps, 'I've been running.'

'I can see that. But why? Calm yourself. Tell me what's happened to you. And tell me why you've come to me and not to your mother.'

Mary looks at him. Slowly recovering her breath she says, 'I've something to tell you.' Then she turns so pale that he thinks she is about to faint. Her lips quiver and her eyes shine with unshed tears.

'Mary, what is it? What's wrong?' Joseph cannot understand why this young woman, whom he knows to be normally so serene, has become so agitated.

Looking down at the hands she is clasping and unclasping in her lap, Mary whispers, 'I went up into the mountains, to our favourite place, you know, beside the great cedar tree we love so much. I went to sing praises to the God of Abraham and to think about all the wonderful things the rabbi said in the synagogue. About the joy a righteous wife brings to her husband. About how a good wife is better than rubies. I want to be the very best wife to you, Joseph,' Mary says, blinking at him and smiling faintly. 'The air was cool and clear, full of the scent of lilies, cedar and pinewood. And then, something wonderful happened. It was…' Mary breaks off, and stares into space as if she can see, even now, her mountain refuge.

'It was… I don't know how to describe it. The wind was rustling in the trees and whispering through the grasses; and the birds were singing to one another as if it was daybreak, and then… I felt a presence with me. It was so real I was a little afraid. I looked all round but there was no one. I felt light-headed, as though I had not eaten, so I lay down and closed my eyes. The presence seemed to come closer. I was sure that if I opened my eyes I could see and touch it. So I opened my eyes and still there was no one there. I wondered if it was you, Joseph, hiding from me, to tease me. But I knew that was not possible.'

She stares straight ahead, into the woodpile, seeming to forget Joseph's presence.

'And...?'

She starts, as if waking from a dream. 'Oh, yes. And then... then, I think I fell asleep.'

'You fell asleep?'

'Well, yes. I think I must have fallen asleep. It was all very strange. You see,' and now Mary turns to look fully into Joseph's eyes. Her next words come swiftly, tumbling out on top of one another because she is afraid she may forget what it is she has to say.

'You see, Joseph, I saw a man, bright and shining, dressed all in white, and he smiled at me and called me blessed and said that I would have a baby, very soon, a very special baby. Not like any other baby. Special. I have been chosen...'

Joseph's jaw clenches hard and his massive hands ball into white-knuckled fists. 'What are you saying? Explain yourself!'

Mary, frightened by his reaction, says again, 'I am going to have a baby—soon. A special baby. A boy. A gift from the God of Abraham.'

'Hush, Mary. Be careful of what you are saying.'

'But it's true, Joseph. It's true. And it's wonderful!'

Joseph is beside himself and can barely refrain from striking her, not so much because of the news she brings, bad as it is, but because of her apparent lack of shame. She almost seems to be revelling in her shocking news.

'Wonderful? For shame, girl! What are you saying? Who is this man who has bewitched you. What madness has taken hold of you, up there on the mountain?'

'Madness? No! Oh, no! It is not madness, Joseph. You should have seen the man. You would understand. He was not bad. He was beautiful. More beautiful than any man I have ever seen.'

Joseph cannot refrain from shaking her.

'Who was he? Where is he from? Was it someone from the village? Tell me!'

'He said his name was Gabriel.'

'Gabriel? Where is he from?'

'He didn't tell me. He just said he was a messenger from the Holy One of Israel.'

'You lay with this stranger when you are promised to me?' Joseph shouts, unable to contain himself.

'No! You don't understand. I would not lie with any man, Joseph. How could you think such a thing?' And to Joseph's consternation, Mary bursts into tears. He begins to wonder if she really understands what she is saying. Has some madness indeed taken possession of her?

'You tell me you are with child and you tell me you have not lain with any man! Such a thing is not possible.' Bewildered by his outraged anger Mary gasps, stops crying and opens her eyes wide. At last she understands the full meaning behind his words. The stranger was so real to her that it has not occurred to her that Joseph would not believe her. She has not considered how unlikely her story might sound.

'He was so real.' She speaks less confidently now. 'I saw him. I heard him. But... perhaps I was asleep after all. Perhaps it was a dream?' She closes her eyes, frowning hard. She shakes her head slowly from side to side. 'I don't think it was a dream, Joseph. Something has happened to me.'

'You are expecting a child?'

'Yes Joseph, I am.'

Trying to contain his exasperation Joseph asks again, 'And who is the father of your child, Mary?'

Mary is crying again. 'I do not know. I do not know!'

Joseph has never experienced Mary in such a perverse mood and he finds it infuriating. But, furious though he is, his anger is tempered by his overwhelming love for Mary. Foolish she may be but he is still concerned for her welfare. He is convinced that in her innocence she must have been cunningly seduced or, a more terrible thought occurs to him, taken by force. But how, in that case, to explain her apparent delight when she came to tell him the news? Trying to control his feeling he says, more gently, 'Mary you must tell me who is responsible for this terrible thing. He must understand that it is his responsibility to marry you. I will end our betrothal quietly.'

'End it... divorce me?' Mary is scandalized. 'But Joseph, we are legally bound to each other!'

'You cannot expect me to marry you now that you carry another man's seed.' Joseph is torn between anger, love and confusion that Mary could even think their betrothal might continue. 'How could you think it possible?'

'I thought you loved me!'

'I do love you. Of course I love you. But you have betrayed my love. Surely you understand that?'

'No, no! I don't understand it at all. I thought you would understand.' With these words Mary leaps up from the stool and rushes out of the workshop, running as fast as she can back to the hillside where she has so recently met her wonderful, shining stranger, sobbing hysterically as she goes.

LOVE ALWAYS HOPES

When she is gone, Joseph stares after her. He feels as if a Roman scourge has flayed him. He can hardly believe the encounter he has just had with his bride-to-be. But he has to accept the truth, hard as it is to bear. Leaving on one side the length of wood on his workbench he storms to the corner of his workshop and begins to chop wood furiously. The sweat pours from his body as he raises and swings the axe, up and over and down, thud, up and over and down, thud. The sound of splitting wood resounds throughout the courtyard outside, and beyond.

Finally he sinks exhausted on to the floor on a bed of sawdust and drifts into a fitful sleep. It is night when he awakes to the voice of his mother calling him to supper. He feels around in the darkness for his lamp and, fumbling to light it, makes his way to the house. Here his widowed mother, unaware of the tragic events yet sensing that all is not well, has meat and vegetables stewing over the open fire.

'You have been working late,' is all she says as she ladles a generous serving into a dish and hands it to him with a portion of bread. He does not answer but accepts the food and begins to eat. His mother looks at his exhausted face and says nothing. Whatever troubles him, he will solve his problems for himself, of that she is confident. Besides, she will pray to the Lord God of Abraham, as is her habit. She is certain the God of Abraham will never desert her son because he is a devout man, a descendant of the house of David, beloved of the Lord.

Over the next few days Joseph and Mary do not meet but go about their duties taking care to avoid contact with each other. So it is that the villagers become aware of a cloud hanging over the community. A cloud of uncertainty which grows darker when Mary rises early one morning to visit her elderly cousin, Elizabeth, who lives in the distant province of Judea. The old lady is ailing, they are told, and needs a companion.

Joseph continues to shut himself away in his workshop. He has spoken with Mary's mother, Anna, and with her father, Joachim. It is agreed that he should divorce her privately. Neither of her parents know who is responsible for her shame and it has been agreed that she should remain with her cousin, at least until the baby is born. When Joseph is not busy in his workshop he disappears for hours, walking the surrounding hills and valleys, searching for choice trees to fell. So it is believed. In fact he retreats to the mountains to nurse his baffled grief and rage.

Early one morning, on one of these lonely walks, a mist descends, engulfing him. The familiar landmarks are obscured and to his consternation he realizes that, although in well-known terrain, he is lost. Disorientated he quickens his pace, peering into the mist that envelops him and penetrates the folds of his cloak. He comes to a niche in the side of the mountain and, overcome with exhaustion, he crouches in its shelter to rest. He sleeps. He dreams.

In his dream he hears a loud voice saying, 'I am Gabriel. I stand in the presence of God. The prophecies are true—out of Bethlehem a ruler will come, one whose origins go back to the distant past. He will born of a virgin, conceived by the Holy Spirit of God. Stand up, man, and open your eyes!'

And, in his dream, Joseph is surrounded by a light so dazzling he has to shield his eyes. He can just make out the shape of a man and, scrambling to his feet, hears the thunderous voice continue.

'Mary, your betrothed, is the chosen one. Do not be afraid to marry her. She will have a son and you are to call him Jesus, because he will save his people from their sins.'

Joseph is trying to see the man but the voice is so loud and the light so bright that his senses are overwhelmed.

He wakes abruptly, finding himself prostrate on the ground, and it takes him a while to gather his wits. He does not know where he is, what he is doing here or whether it is evening or morning. He remembers the stranger—the man, Gabriel—and looks around for him. Where is he? He seemed so real. Was it only a dream? Very slowly he recalls the memory of the mysterious mist that engulfed him and turns over in his mind everything he has heard and seen. Mary... chosen... a son... Jesus. What can it all mean?

And then, being a devout man, he raises his hands heavenwards in prayer. He has no doubt that an angel of the Lord did indeed visit Mary, and has now spoken to him. The wonder of it!

It is not long before the village gossips are busy again. Mary has left, very suddenly and somewhat secretly, although it is now known that her cousin in Judea is expecting a baby. Soon after, Joseph also leaves—to go after her, they say. He leaves instructions with his mother and with Anna that they are to arrange for the marriage ceremony to take place as soon as he returns with Mary. And so, on their return, the celebrations begin. The whole community gathers to eat and drink, sing and dance, and join wholeheartedly in wishing health and happiness to the young couple. For a week they celebrate and it is a joyful time—though not without some whispers behind closed doors.

'Mary is looking well,' they say.

'The air in Judea agreed with her.'

'See how plump she has become!'

There is no need now to ask why Mary appeared so pale and with-drawn in the days before she set off to visit her cousin. Some wear a smug air, secretly amused that the families of Joseph and Joachim, for all their righteous observance of the Law, are no more above human weakness than their illustrious ancestor, the great King David. But there is no malice in the gossip and all are delighted that the affair has ended happily and that the young couple has respected tradition by asking their neighbours to witness their union in marriage.

In fact, there is little time for further speculation because, even before the feasting is over, alarming news reaches them. Roman soldiers are marching towards the village. When they arrive they bring news that Caesar Augustus has issued a decree that a census is to be taken of the entire Roman world. For this each man must return to his birthplace, together with his family and household. While most of the villagers have been born and bred in Galilee the census still creates an unwelcome disruption to their tranquil lives. But for others, Joseph and Joachim among them, it is a great upheaval. They must make the long trek back to Jerusalem. To undertake this pilgrimage for one of the great religious feasts is a joy; to make the arduous journey on the whim of a foreign power creates general resentment. But a Roman decree cannot be ignored. The roads are full of travellers, many of them being of the Davidic line, trudging their way to Jerusalem. Once more Joseph and Mary, this time together as man and wife, and now accompanied by their families, set out for Jerusalem.

OUT OF EGYPT

Many months have passed since Mary and Joseph started out, newly wed, on their journey south to the city of David, leaving the hills of Galilee behind. But their journey does not end in Jerusalem. Events occur which cause them to flee further south, following the footsteps of the patriach Joseph, to the land of Egypt. Here they now live, with their little son, as exiles, refugees, far from home and in a foreign land.

Mary, on the rooftop of the house where they lodge, sings to herself as she stoops over the drying flax. She turns the coarse bundles, carefully gathering those that are ready to beat and separate. These she will spin into a fine thread, ready for weaving into soft linen. Some of this she will sell in the market-place but she will keep back enough to make a delicate tunic for her little son. She and Joseph are content to wear the usual cotton garments of their class, but for her son only the best linen will do. Since arriving she has learnt to value the Egyptian skill of rotting the flax before beating it, but she is less at ease with other customs in this alien land. Especially she dislikes the women's use of cosmetics, their heavily oiled hair, and heady perfumes. She feels uncomfortable with the men's strange custom of shaving the hair from their faces. The high officials even shave their heads, making them look very strange. Many of her own people, having lived here for generations, have adopted these peculiar customs. She longs to return to her own country but she keeps her melancholy to herself. She does not want to worry Joseph and the child.

Above everything else she wants to create a serene and happy home for her husband and son. Indeed, despite the trivial irritations and the homesickness of her exile, laughter and singing fill the home.

Singing now to herself on the rooftop, she hears Joseph below, choosing the wood for his next day's work, moving quietly about the courtyard, so as not to wake the sleeping child. He has more work than he can easily manage, rising at dawn and working steadily until dusk every day. The only exception to this is the Sabbath, when they join the small band of like-minded believers in their displaced community and attend the modest local synagogue.

For the most part the Egyptians have welcomed Joseph and Mary warmly into their community. They find the appearance and manners of their new neighbours strange and unsophisticated, but they recognize Joseph's exceptional knowledge of wood, and his skill as a master carpenter. In Egypt, a land where fine wood is scarce, men who know how to choose and craft the best trees are highly valued. This strange Judean becomes a familiar figure at the quayside when the ships arrive from the forests of Lebanon. Often his small son is perched upon his shoulders, clutching his father's head and questioning him eagerly about the ships and the sailors and the land of Lebanon where trees grow as high as houses, beyond Galilee, his parents' home.

'But why did you leave, Father?'

'Because of the Roman census, my son.'

'Why did you not return?'

'We shall return, my son.'

'When, Father? When shall we return?'

'At the appointed time.'

'When will that be?'

'I do not know,' his father answers patiently.

'Then, how will you know?' the child persists, puzzled.

'God will tell me,' his father answers with a smile.

'How will he tell you, Father?'

Laughing at his son's insistence, Joseph explains, 'My son, an angel of the Lord will come to me and tell me when the time is right. Meanwhile we must be patient. We must live here and do the work we have been given to do until the time of the angel's appearing.'

The child says nothing more but he wonders about his father's words. An angel of the Lord! He longs to return to the land of his birth, yet he is here, in the land of Egypt. He knows that his forefathers settled here, in this land, hundreds and hundreds and hundreds of years ago. His mother and his father have told him wonderful stories of his ancestors, how they came to live here, of their captivity and escape, of their wanderings in the wilderness until they were delivered. And of how they went to live in the land flowing with milk and honey—his homeland. Because it is so fertile, it is always a troubled land, and even now is occupied by soldiers of the Roman Empire. How he longs to go there!

The small boy adores his father and loves to be with him as he works. His eyes rarely leave the carpenter's face but he knows better than to speak while his father sits silently, studying a huge block of uncut wood. This is a time to be as quiet and still as a cat. By careful observation the child, young as he is, knows the precise moment when a sharp gleam in his father's eye precedes a long intake of breath. Still the child knows he must not speak. Not until the axe is raised high over his father's head and brought down hard, splitting the wood in two, and three, and more; not until the careful work of crafting proper is begun, does he dare to ask, 'What is it to be, Father?'

And so the conversation begins, and the stories are told, and the lessons of life are learned.

He loves to watch his mother at work, too. One day, as she turns the millstone to grind the corn, he asks, 'Mother, do you miss your homeland?'

'Yes, I do. But why do you ask?'

'You are so happy, and you sing all the time. Don't you feel sad to be so far from home?'

She laughs. 'I don't know how to explain to it you, but I will try. When you are grown up you will understand better. I miss my home and my family and friends. I miss the places I know and the familiar ways of my people and I long to return to them. But our God brought us as strangers to this land, even as he brought our forefather Joseph so many years ago. He is with us here, just as he was with Joseph, and he knows what is best for us. And when the time is right we shall return.'

'One day. That's what Father said. He said an angel of the Lord would tell him when the time is right for us to go home.'

Mary smiles. 'And so he will.'

'How do you know? Have you ever seen an angel, Mother?'

'Yes, my son. I have.'

'Oh! Tell me about it. Please do!'

Mary lifts her eyes from the millstone and her hands are still as she looks long and searchingly at her son, the suggestion of a frown on her young face. Slowly she speaks.

'It was a long time ago, before you were born. High on the hills of Galilee, before I was married to your father, Gabriel, the angel of the Lord, came to me and said I would have a son.' Mary looks at the boy. The child waits impatiently. His mother's face tells him there is much more to come, but it also warns him not to ask. They are both so intense in their shared silence that neither of them hears Joseph approach.

'Well, what strange power has taken hold of my home that I find you both in a trance?' he asks jovially.

'Oh Father. Mother was just telling me about how she met the angel Gabriel.'

'What a boy you are for asking questions,' his father says, bending down to jab him playfully in the ribs, but the child giggles and evades his father's hand.

'There will be time enough for talk of angels when you are older. Just now there is time for a swim before your mother serves up our meal. Come now, let's be away to the river.'

Mary watches them go before turning again to her work. She recalls the words Gabriel spoke to her.

You are to give him the name Jesus. He will be great and will be called the Son of the Most High. God will give him the throne of his father David.' She recalls too the words of the prophet, '*Out of Egypt I called my son.*'

Not for the first time the awesome power of God in the fulfilling of his purposes takes her breath away. She remembers the terrible moment when Joseph, returning grim-faced from the quayside, told her of the news brought to him from their homeland. Herod had ordered the massacre of every male child under the age of two years. It happened soon after the angel warned Joseph in a dream to escape to Egypt with his wife and infant son. At first the terrible news didn't make sense to them. She and Joseph had knelt together to thank God for delivering their son, and wept in agony as they thought about the slaughter and suffering of their friends and neighbours. It pained them as they sat together long into the evening, each turning over in their minds what it could mean. It was with an uncomfortable mixture of horror and relief that they began to understand that it was their son, their own baby, that Herod had been intent upon slaying.

'Who is this child given so wonderfully into our care? Who are we to carry so great a responsibility? We are not fit for the task, and yet… it is the work we have been given to do.'

It seems so long ago, that day on the mountain when the angel first appeared to her. Yes, and the ecstasy of her son's birth and the extraordinary visit of the shepherds with their story of a brilliant light, and angels singing. Then the visit of the wise men from the east, and their extravagant gifts. Then the dream and the warning. She cherishes all these secret memories.

On an impulse she quickly wipes her hands and hurries to the storeroom. Taking out some carefully wrapped old clothes which she lays on the floor, she thoughtfully unwraps the jewelled casket hidden deep inside the bundle. Holding her breath she opens the lid to gaze at the exquisite gold filigree bracelets, necklaces, ornaments and coins which glitter in the dim light. This is treasure given to them by the eastern strangers—wealth beyond their wildest dreams. But its real value to her is that it is tangible proof of the presence of the Holy One of Israel in their home, and because it represents the miracle of their son's birth, the visits of the angel, the shepherds and the eastern sages. Now she lifts out a beautifully carved and inlaid wooden box containing myrrh, and she remembers the blessing of the old man, Simeon, in the temple at Jerusalem when he saw her newborn son.

'This child is destined to cause the falling and rising of many in Israel, and to be a sign that will be spoken against, so that the thoughts of many hearts will be revealed. And a sword will pierce your own soul too.'

She sits for a while, gently running her fingers over the polished surface of the box, pondering once more the mysteries surrounding her precious son.

The next morning Joseph wakes Mary from sleep. His eyes have a contented gleam she has not seen for a long time.

'We are going home,' he says. 'The angel came last night. Those who were trying to take the child's life are dead. We can go home.'

They hold each other in a tight embrace and Mary laughs and cries with delight. The child, Jesus, woken by the commotion, calls out to know what is happening.

'We are going home, my son,' Mary tells him through laughter and tears. 'The angel has come and we are going home.'

PRAYER

Lord Jesus Christ,
who has called us to a costly discipleship,
help us to live with integrity
in every circumstance of life.
Grant us wisdom and courage
to heed the voice of angels,
and always to live with hope and love.
Amen

CHAPTER EIGHT

THE PRISONER
AND HIS WIFE

'Simon, Simon, Satan has asked to sift you as wheat. But I have prayed for you, Simon, that your faith may not fail. And when you have turned back, strengthen your brothers.'
LUKE 22:31

In this you greatly rejoice, though now for a little while you may have had to suffer grief in all kinds of trials. These have come so that your faith—of greater worth than gold, which perishes even though refined by fire—may be proved genuine and may result in praise, glory and honour when Jesus Christ is revealed. Though you have not seen him, you love him; and even though you do not see him now, you believe in him and are filled with an inexpressible and glorious joy, for you are receiving the goal of your faith, the salvation of your souls.
1 PETER 1:6–8

IN THE DUNGEON

A prisoner, worn with age, shivers in the dungeon beneath the Tower of Antonia in Jerusalem. In the gloom, lit only by a smouldering torch set into an iron bracket, he cannot distinguish night from day. In the silence, only the sound of water dripping from the dank walls punctuates the passing of time. Sometimes he hears other unseen captives, groaning in agony or uttering deranged cries, having spent too long in this dreadful twilight world. The pitiful man, aged beyond his years by a life of toil, shudders in the darkness, and tries to draw his woollen cloak more closely round his shoulders. But his efforts are frustrated by the heavy chains that anchor him in place. These chains are wound around his wrists and secured at each end to his jailers, two burly soldiers, who sleep on either side of him. Stupefied with cheap wine they snore heavily, their stinking breath adding to the reeking odour of the dungeon.

Incarceration is a punishment for guards and prisoner alike. The guards are allotted the duty for minor insubordination. The prisoner, however, is chained for a very different offence. He is here for displaying unshakeable loyalty—loyalty and unquestioning obedience to an unseen Commander. A Commander martyred many years ago but who yet lives. Lives in those who, like the prisoner, have absolute confidence in him. Some indeed have seen him and spoken to him since he died but others, not seeing but believing, know the reality of his power in their lives. Such is the faith of these believers and such is their devotion to their unseen Commander that the prisoner, Simon Peter, being one of their leaders, has become a threat to the Establishment—the Roman rulers and the leaders of the Jews. The prisoner's faith and confidence are all-consuming. He no longer trusts in the Law alone, nor in a doctrine or a creed, but in a living being. How can this be? This is the question that disturbs, and this is the reason Simon Peter, God's fisherman, lies here shackled and shivering in this living hell.

Peter does not know how long he has been here. Not long, surely? Yet it seems like an eternity. And why is he here? In his weakened state, hungry and parched with thirst, his brain begins to play tricks. He thinks he can hear a cock crowing in the distance, and a voice, faint but insistent: 'Before the cock crows... three times... three times... three times.'

He is gripped by terror. What will happen three times? No! He will not listen. Relentlessly the voice continues, echoing inside his head: 'You will deny me. Deny me.'

Now he remembers. Jesus... his Teacher... his Friend.

'I do not know him.' And he remembers his fear, his curses, and his shame. And his friend, Jesus, turning... bruised body, bound limbs, blood-spattered face... looking directly at him.

Tears of remorse spill from his bloodshot eyes and trickle down his wrinkled face. Groans of denial once more escape him. 'No...I will not deny him... I will not... I will not deny him!'

'But you did!' Another voice, clear, strong and harsh, startles Simon Peter from his confused reverie. He gasps. Now he is awake, his mind no longer clouded.

'Who's that? Who's there?' He peers into the gloom. The guards continue to snore. 'Who spoke to me?' Simon Peter demands.

There is no answer. Now the very silence seems to mock him. He feels a presence in the darkness, some malevolent force intent to do him harm. Suddenly he is afraid with a terror he has never before experienced in his turbulent life as a fisherman, a disciple or a prisoner. A void lies before him and he is being inexorably drawn towards it.

'Save me! Lord, save me!'

His whole being is in the cry but only a low moan escapes his parched lips. But even as it does he hears the first voice again, but clearer now, the voice of one he loves—Jesus. Jesus is saying once more as he said long ago, 'You of little faith, why do you doubt?'

And Simon Peter remembers. He is in a boat with his friends again. It is night, and there is a terrible storm. The waves toss the boat high in the air and dash it down again. An apparition appears on the sea. They are afraid but Simon Peter says, 'It is the Teacher. It is Jesus.'

'No. How could a man walk on water?' the others retort.

'It is him, I'm sure of it,' Simon Peter answers. He calls out, 'Lord, if it really is you, tell me to come to join you.'

'Come,' the ghostly figure says.

Peter leaps out of the boat and, amazing himself and his companions, begins to approach Jesus. Neither he nor the others can believe what is happening. Then Simon Peter feels the fury of the wind, looks down at the waves crashing around him, and begins to sink. He cries out in a panic, 'Lord, save me!'

And Jesus stretches out his hand and catches him, saying, 'You of little faith, why do you doubt?'

As he relives this event, Simon Peter sees Jesus again, standing here once more, looking at him. In desolation Peter reaches out his hand to his

Teacher and Friend. Immediately the vision vanishes, but the terror has gone and Simon Peter is now calm. New life courses through his old body and he is strong once more. He is at peace... dreaming.

He smells the sea. He sees a fire and feels the warmth of the glowing embers. He smells fish roasting and hears it sizzling. And there are the well-loved hands of his Master, so precious, breaking bread, slowly, carefully, thoughtfully, then...

Three times. Three times. Three times...

'Simon, son of John.' Now the voice is no more than a whisper on the air, like the first gentle breath of spring. 'Do you love me? Do you love me? Do you truly love me?'

'Yes, my Lord,' Peter murmurs. 'You know I do.'

'Feed my lambs.'

Dreaming still, Peter smiles into the darkness and remembers their last conversation. Jesus had told him that in his old age he would lose his independence and find himself at the mercy of others. But the command was the same as it had been all those years before when, mending his nets, he raised his head, met the eyes of Jesus and heard the words 'Follow me'.

Now Peter sees the face of his wife Miriam smiling at him. In that moment he feels her presence so near and so real that he stretches out a trembling hand towards her, even as he had stretched out his hand to Jesus. She is saying, 'My dear! My love! I am here. The Lord is with us. Do not fret. He will deliver you.'

In his confused mind he is with her once more on that Sabbath day, watching as she bends over the near-lifeless body of her much-loved mother. He sees the tears falling on to the cold white face. He sees Miriam holding her mother's limp hand, stroking it, and he hears her crying quietly. Her mother has the fever which has claimed so many lives. As he watches and listens, feeling so helpless, Jesus comes into the house. He has no fear of the fever but takes the hand of the sick woman. And... she is well. She is preparing a meal for them, and Miriam is saying, 'All is well. Come and eat.'

IN THE UPPER ROOM

Shadows cast by the flickering oil lamps dance upon the walls of the crowded room. It is a small room in an upper storey of a narrow street, in the occupied city of Jerusalem, but a diverse group has taken shelter here. Mothers hush little children, who cling anxiously to their skirts; fathers and young men stand on guard, tense and listening. In the distance they can hear soldiers drawing near, their feet thudding along the paved street and their loud voices echoing in the confined space. They are shouting insults against the inhabitants of the city. Their words are foreign but their meaning is unmistakable. The irregularity of their stomping feet, their slurred obscenities and raucous laughter leave no doubt as to their intoxicated state. They approach slowly, drunkenly, but inexorably.

In the stillness of the upper room people are thinking of James, the brother of John. James, their leader, who walked with Jesus. James who had gone to the synagogue every day and, throwing caution to the winds, had fearlessly and passionately told the story of Jesus, the Messiah, the risen One, the living One. So powerfully did he speak that many who heard believed. But then the authorities, fearing a rebellion and hoping to make an example of James, arrested him and executed him. And now they have also arrested Simon. How long before he too is executed? Perhaps he has been executed already! Who is there to take his place and to lead and teach the small but growing band of followers of Jesus, the Christ? Can they survive without Simon Peter's strength and vision? They have been unable to visit him and they have no news of him. If he is still alive they know his jailors will not feed him and they are worried for his well-being.

They have gathered together in this place to pray for his deliverance, but the agonizing questions in every heart, which only a few dare express, hang heavily in the air.

'Why should Simon Peter be spared when James was not?'

'The Lord himself was not delivered, but he rose again from death.'

'It is not so for his disciples. None of those killed has been seen alive.'

'Many have been killed. What purpose has been served by their sacrifice?'

'What has happened to the mighty working of the Spirit, the coming of power upon each one of us on the day of Pentecost?'

'Has it all been for nothing?'

'No, of course not. How could it be?'

'We still have the Spirit present with us.'

'Yes.'

'Yes, of course. It will be all right.'

Each of them wrestles with private doubts and fears. Each one believes the others to be stronger in their faith. This is why they have gathered together—to draw strength from one another and to cling to a hope which individually they do not possess. In the hidden places of their hearts, they all doubt. In meeting together to talk and to pray, they speak with a confidence they do not feel. Some pray, secretly, 'Lord, help my unbelief.'

And others cry quietly, 'Why have you forsaken us?'

And some cry aloud, 'Have mercy upon us, O Lord, and deliver us from our distress.'

Now another voice is heard, speaking with quiet confidence. It is Simon Peter's wife, Miriam.

'Have you forgotten the song of David?' She begins to sing and, old though she is, her voice is as clear as a bell and as sound as that of a woman half her age.

'God is our shepherd and he will guide us to springs of living water. He will comfort and refresh us. He will wipe away all tears from our eyes. We shall want for nothing…'

As Miriam sings the prayer of the shepherd-king, the others join in one by one, gaining courage as they sing. But even as they sing they hear the soldiers' footsteps again, coming closer and closer. Some of the women hug one another for comfort, some clutch each other's hands, and some clasp their hands in prayer. The men sit silent and alert, heads inclined, listening, ready for any eventuality. The pounding feet are louder… hearts beat faster. The muttered oaths and heavy breathing of the conscripts can be heard through the wooden door. Then, the footsteps pass. There is an audible sigh of relief and the terrified group relaxes. On this occasion at least, they are safe.

Gradually conversation begins to flow once more. The children, aware that danger has passed, begin to squabble among themselves. One of the women cries out, 'Praise be to the God of Jesus, of Abraham and of Moses, for this night we have been spared.'

'But for how long?' another asks.

'We must trust God. He will make his way plain.'

'Yes, but how many of us must perish in the doing of it?'

'How can the purposes of God be fulfilled by so many deaths?'

'We should flee and join the believers at Tarsus, or even go south, to Alexandria.'

'The women and children perhaps, but not the men.'

'We should fight!'

Now Miriam, Simon Peter's wife, speaks again, calm, composed and tranquil. 'This is not the way the Master taught us,' she says. 'Don't you remember how he rebuked my husband for raising his sword against the High Priest's servant?'

'True, Miriam, but he didn't say we should never fight.' John, the brother of James, speaks. 'Don't you remember that he warned us that he had not come to bring peace, but a sword? He cautioned us that he would set son against father and daughter against mother. Don't you remember? Surely this was what he was preparing us to do. Surely the time has come for us to take up arms.'

'Against the might of Rome?'

'It is impossible! We cannot fight Rome.'

'Neither can we hide away.'

'Remember the day of Pentecost,' one of the men says now. 'Remember the power that came upon us so that we were overwhelmed with a strength and wisdom beyond our understanding. That same Holy Spirit of power is ours for the asking.'

'But should we use that power to take up arms against Rome? Is that really what the Master wanted?'

'If that was his intention, why didn't he save himself when he was on the cross? If such power was available to him, why didn't he lead us in the battle to overthrow the Imperialists? That was what Judas Iscariot wanted.'

'But it was not what Jesus intended. Don't you remember? He said, "My kingdom is not of this world."'

'What did he mean?'

'Simon Peter would know,' John says softly.

'Don't you know? You were as close to the Master as he was!'

'Yes, but it was Simon whom the Master named Peter, the rock. He was the one called to take charge and shepherd the flock. That's why we need him here. We need him as much as our ancestors needed Moses to guide them through the wilderness.'

'We must pray for guidance. Don't you remember what Jesus said? "Where two or three are gathered in my name, I am in the midst of them."'

'And what if Simon is already beheaded, like James?' This from Thomas, who has not spoken before.

'He will not be,' says Miriam, calmly.

'How do you know?' Thomas asks.

'I don't know. But I feel it.'

'James was fearless and he preached the truths of God everywhere he went. We should do the same.'

'And suffer the same fate? How can that bring the kingdom of God to earth?'

'I don't know.'

Now Mary, the mother of Jesus, speaks. Until now she has been silent, listening to all that has been said. Every eye turns to the corner where she sits beside the fire.

'Thomas,' she says, 'have you forgotten so soon? Don't you remember putting your finger into the scars on my son's hands? My son who was crucified by the Romans. My son, who has risen, who has ascended to his Father. My son who sent the Holy Spirit of God upon us. And why? So that we might live to continue his work here on earth. Let us all pray to the Father of our Lord Jesus that the Holy Spirit will quicken our minds. Let us recall all that Jesus did and said among us. Let us remind ourselves of his teaching and of all his works. John Mark, you write it down. And you too, Dr Luke, you can record everything. Then, perhaps as we remember and record these truths, the way ahead will become clear to us.'

There are murmurs of assent and, with the release of tension, the women bustle about to set a low table in the centre of the room, collect barley loaves and jugs of wine.

'We will celebrate the agape meal,' Miriam says, 'just as Jesus taught on his last night, to remember him.'

Solemnly, the whole company gathers in a circle and John, the brother of the martyred James, takes the loaves, blesses them and breaks them, saying, 'In doing this we remember our last meal with our beloved Master, and we give thanks.' Then John passes the broken loaves to the assembled company. He takes a jug of wine and, giving thanks for the life and death and rising again of Jesus, their Friend and Teacher, he drinks from it. As each eats the bread and drinks the wine, a new mood inspires the company. Hope replaces fear and despondency.

THE VISITOR

While his friends are sharing bread and wine together, Simon Peter has fallen into a deep and peaceful sleep. And Miriam, his wife, comes to him in a dream. He sees her smile and offer him bread. He takes it and eats, and it is sweet-tasting and nourishing. He feels new strength surge through his limbs. Now Miriam offers him a cup filled with the very best wine. He takes it from her and drinks deeply. All the while she is smiling at him, her head inclined towards him tenderly. Her eyes are speaking to him without words: 'Have no fear,' they are saying, 'only believe. The Master is with you. He will deliver you. Remember the scriptures, my husband, where it is written that the Lord our God is always with us. We cannot be defeated because he is close beside us. He is our rest, our hope and our strength.'

Her presence is so real that he reaches out to stroke the beloved face. The face which has grown old with him so that in every line he can trace the history of her devotion. From the earliest days when he first made sacrifices to follow Jesus, through those three tumultuous years of travelling and preaching, and in all the years since, she has accompanied him without complaining. Sometimes Simon Peter thinks that the faith and conviction of Miriam is even stronger than his own. He does not believe that she would ever have denied knowing the Master. And yet... he has never told her so. He is overwhelmed with remorse that he has not told Miriam how much he loves her and how much he values her patient confidence in every situation. Now he longs for an opportunity to tell her.

Suddenly, even as he dreams of his wife, a brilliant light dazzles him. He tries to shield his eyes but he cannot move. Then someone taps him sharply on his side and a voice says, 'Quick! Wake up! Get up!'

With that, the chains fall off Simon Peter's wrists. This is truly a remarkable dream. It seems so real. He raises his arms and he is no longer shackled to his guards.

'Put on your cloak and sandals!'

Bewildered, Peter obeys, hoping he will not wake up—hoping he will soon see Miriam once more.

'Now, follow me!' the voice commands and, in a trance, Peter does so. He follows the shining figure of a man, which moves ahead of him. The figure leads him to the first heavy door of the dungeon and it opens soundlessly. They pass through and come to another heavily bolted and guarded door. Once more the rusty hinges silently swing open. The figure moves on through dark passages and up steep stairways. They come at last to an iron gate that, yet again, opens mysteriously, noiselessly, and Simon Peter finds himself in the street. Still hoping not to wake up he follows his guide. He is cold and draws his cloak closer. This dream is more real than any other, and with a sense of wonder he believes he must be dying.

Then, weakened by days of starvation, his footsteps falter. He stubs his toe and curses aloud. In that instant the shining figure disappears.

'No, don't go!' Simon Peter cries out. 'Don't go! Don't leave me here!'

He hears his voice ring out into the night. He glances down at his feet. He lifts his head to gaze at the stone wall beside him. Slowly he stretches out his hand. He touches it. The wall is cold and wet and solid.

Now, his hand still thrust upon the wall to give him support, he looks up the street ahead of him then turns round to survey the street behind him.

'It's not a dream! It's not a dream!' he whispers. 'I'm free!' Astounded Simon Peter catches his breath.

'I'm free!' he says again. 'It was an angel! It was not a dream. I'm free! Oh, Miriam, Miriam. Your prayers have been answered. I'm free and I'm coming to you. I have been spared to serve a little longer.'

Laughing and crying, Peter begins to hurry along the now familiar streets to his home, where Miriam and all their friends are waiting and praying earnestly for him.

THE WELCOME

Thud! Thud! Thud!

The prayers are interrupted by the sudden loud noise at the outer door. The hammering is insistent. Loud. Urgent.

Simon Peter's wife lifts her head. The movement, slight as it is, reveals her courage and unshaken faith. It is as if she has looked into the abyss and seen light glimmering in the darkness.

'Someone is knocking, Rhoda,' she says. 'Go down to the door and see who it is.'

The company is astonished by her composure. Rhoda, the servant girl, does not move. She is shivering with fright and begins to whimper.

Encouraged by Miriam's example, John speaks. 'Do as Miriam says, Rhoda. Calm yourself and answer the door. Remember the Spirit of God is with us. He will not desert us. All of us here are ready to do his will whatever it may be.'

'But,' Rhoda weeps, 'I'm so afraid!'

'We are all afraid,' John replies. 'But we will be given the strength we need... and courage enough to face whatever may await us. So now, go! Answer the door!'

Reluctantly, Rhoda leaves the upper room and makes her way slowly, falteringly, down to the courtyard. Reaching the door she opens it a crack and peers out.

'Who's there?' Her voice squeaks unnaturally. She clears her throat and tries again, 'Hello! Who's there?' Her voice is a mere whisper.

'Rhoda. Don't be afraid. It's me, Simon. Simon called Peter.'

'Oh!' she gasps and slams the door shut.

Shaking and stumbling she rushes back across the courtyard, up the stairs and bursts into the room where the others are waiting. Half-laughing, half-crying she blurts out, 'It's Simon, the rock. Peter... Simon Peter! He's at the door!'

'Pull yourself together, Rhoda,' John Mark sounds angry. On all sides voices are raised indignantly.

'You must be mistaken.'

'Simon Peter is in the dungeon.'

'In the tower of Antonia.'

'They will not release him…'

'…and he cannot escape.'

'He is heavily guarded.'

'But I saw Simon Peter! At the door. I did! He told me he was Simon who is called Peter!'

Just for a moment there is silence in the room. Not the silence induced by fear, as previously, but the silence of disbelief. They are perplexed as if, waking from a deep sleep, they find themselves in an unfamiliar place. The protesting believers, who so recently prayed for their friend to be released from prison and delivered from certain death, are speechless as they look at Rhoda. Clearly, she is convinced of what she has seen. Where then is Peter? Why hasn't he entered the house with her? Someone whispers, 'It must have been his ghost.'

'Yes. It must have been his ghost. They must have executed him already.'

As the full import of these words begins to dawn upon the small company they exchange glances and heads turn to the corner where Simon's wife Miriam is seated. While they are trying to find something to say, Mary, the mother of Jesus, speaks to Rhoda. 'My dear, if Simon Peter is at the door,' she says calmly, 'you had best go back and let the poor man in. He must be hungry. I will prepare a place for him at the table.'

Rhoda seems a long time returning. A breathless, excited anticipation fills the room. Far below, the outer door slams shut. Rapid footsteps are heard below, crossing the courtyard, pausing, continuing. Now Rhoda is climbing the stairs and slower, heavier, hesitant footsteps follow her, coming closer. The door creaks open. Simon Peter is stooping there, barely recognizable. He looks bemused, his clothes and face filthy, his beard matted. Miriam rises from her seat suddenly, shudders, sways, is about to faint, but with an effort steadies herself. What have they done to him? Taking a grip on herself she takes a step forward and reaches out her hand, 'Simon,' she says.

At the sound of his name Simon Peter lifts his head and his eyes search out the voice.

'Miriam.'

The two old people regard each other as the lamps flicker on the faces of those who watch them. Then Simon Peter is in Miriam's arms. Her husband has returned from the valley of the shadow of death.

THE WAY AHEAD

When Simon Peter has washed and eaten and rested, he tells his friends how the angel visited him in prison; how his chains fell off him; how the doors flew open soundlessly whilst the guards slept.

When they are alone and Miriam is lying once more in the arms of her husband she asks him, 'Was it very bad in prison?'

'Yes, it was,' he answers. 'At times I feared I was losing my mind, but though it was a terrible experience, I know I have come out of it a better man. In my darkest hour the Master came to me. His presence strengthened me. I knew there was nothing they could do to me, however painful, however terrible—and it was terrible, Miriam—nothing they could do could separate me from his love.' He pauses, deep in thought, 'It sounds a strange thing to say, but I knew myself loved in that dungeon, Miriam, as I have never known it before. And you, were you very anxious, my dear?'

'I was,' she answers simply. Then, after a while she adds, 'But I poured my heart out before the Lord—all my fears and dreads and anxieties—until there were no words left. Then in the deepest silence I rested in his presence. And, you know, after a while it seemed as if it didn't really matter. My fears and anxieties were still there, somewhere deep inside me, but...' She stops, lost for words.

'But you felt yourself enveloped in love?' her husband whispers.

'Yes. Yes. That's it. I did.'

Wrapped in each other's arms, they sleep.

In the morning the whole company is gathered together.

'I must leave for a safer place. They will come here searching for me and my work is not yet complete,' Peter tells them. 'Next time they take me, as

I am sure they will, there may be no escape. Before that I have letters to write.'

'Letters?' they say.

'Yes,' Peter replies. 'My days are numbered. I know that. For this reason I have to make the best use of the time that is available to me. John Mark, my friend, you are an accomplished scribe. I want you to record all the stories and teachings of Jesus that I will tell you. And I must write to the churches that are scattered abroad. I must tell them what we have learnt so that they will stand firm in the days of persecution that are coming. There is so much to do…

PRAYER

Three-in-One, Creator God,
As we look back over our lives
We thank you
That you have brought us through many trials
To the present moment.

Three-in-One, Redeemer Christ,
For every time we fail to love
Forgive us.
By your death and resurrection
Renew us.

Three-in-One, Spirit God,
In whom we have our being
And our hope.
By the light of your love
Inspire us.
Amen.

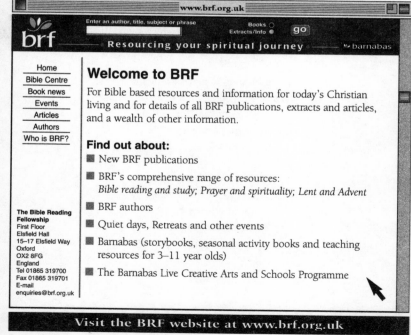

Enter an author, title, subject or phrase

Books ○
Extracts/Info ●

go

brf

Resourcing your spiritual journey — barnabas

Home
Bible Centre
Book news
Events
Articles
Authors
Who is BRF?

**The Bible Reading
Fellowship**
First Floor
Elsfield Hall
15–17 Elsfield Way
Oxford
OX2 8FG
England
Tel 01865 319700
Fax 01865 319701
E-mail
enquiries@brf.org.uk

Welcome to BRF

For Bible based resources and information for today's Christian
living and for details of all BRF publications, extracts and articles,
and a wealth of other information.

Find out about:

■ New BRF publications

■ BRF's comprehensive range of resources:
  Bible reading and study; Prayer and spirituality; Lent and Advent

■ BRF authors

■ Quiet days, Retreats and other events

■ Barnabas (storybooks, seasonal activity books and teaching
  resources for 3–11 year olds)

■ The Barnabas Live Creative Arts and Schools Programme

Visit the BRF website at www.brf.org.uk